A History of
GOATHLAND

THE STORY OF
A MOORLAND COMMUNITY

BY
ALICE HOLLINGS

Goathland, c.1930

First published 1971
Revised and reprinted 1990

Edited by Jill Renney
Designed by Julie Anne Gow: North York Moors National Park
© North York Moors National Park 1990
Printed by AB Printers Limited, Leicester
ISBN 0 907480 26 8

CONTENTS

Tracing Goathland's History

Allice Hollings sets out to give a talk
on village life, c.1970

PREFACE

Alice Hollings was born in 1892 at Hawthorn Hill on Allan Tofts and from early childhood her home was in Beckhole. She went to Goathland School and gained a parish scholarship to Lady Lumley's Grammar School, Pickering, travelling each day by train. After her marriage in 1918 she lived in London but came back frequently with her family. She returned to live permanently in Goathland when her husband retired and continued her intensive research into local history, encouraging many local people to do the same. She was an honorary curator of Whitby Museum, and her research papers and extensive resource notes and maps are deposited in the library of the Whitby Literary and Philosophical Society.

Her book *Goathland — The Story of a Moorland Village* with detailed references was first published in 1971 and has been revised and updated with the assistance of her daughter, Joy Storrs Fox, and Julia Maskens for this edition. It now joins a series of books which have been republished by the National Park to ensure that publications which provide a valuable insight into the local history of the area remain in print.

This edition has been illustrated by photographs which have been kindly loaned by Joy Storrs Fox and Peter Dickinson.

From The Foreword to the First Edition

Many people in Goathland have kindly lent me their house and farm deeds, private papers, accounts and estate maps. Without these, there could not have been such close knowledge of the older generations. I am indebted to them all and also to Mr Smailes for his loan of the village Tithe Map. I also wish to express my thanks to the members of the Goathland Local History Group for the help and encouragement they have given me over so many years.

Alice Hollings
1971

INTRODUCTION

Goathland's history is a fascinating one with an economic and social story stretching back from today over a period of almost 900 years. Before this time place names of Danish, Norse and Celtic origin point to earlier settlements while the horizon is crowned by the *howes* or burial places of Bronze Age folk who lived in the district more than 3000 years ago.

The name Goathland is interesting in itself. It may derive either from *Goda-land*, the settlement of a Dane or Norseman of that name, or from *God-land*, the home of a band of Christian Brothers. The earliest known spelling is *Godeland* in about 1100 but it changes to *Gotheland* by 1296 and, by 1301, appears as *Goyelaunde*.

After the Conquest Goathland was kept in the hands of the king until Henry III gave it to his son Edmund, Earl of Lancaster. In later years it became part of the Duchy of Lancaster in the inheritance of the Crown. Consequently, Goathland is different from many villages in that it never had a manor house with a lord looking after his people, or a rectory where people of better education lived who could have been a contact with the outside world. From its beginning it was a widely scattered peasant community.

One has only to look down on the narrow dale from above to realise how marginal the land is, and what continual management and unceasing toil is necessary to prevent it returning to its original state of scrub and forest.

Recent agricultural returns show thirty-three holdings which were originally ploughed out of the ground of the ancient forest of Pickering. The number of these has only increased by five since 1500. Until 1845 when a steam railway line linking the village with York took the place of a horse-drawn line between Whitby and Pickering, agriculture and work dependent on it was the only economy. With the advent of the steam line the old self-contained village economy slowly disappeared. Today its isolation is diminished even further. Thousands of visitors share the peace of the moors and the rich history of the dale with local people, some of whom can trace their ancestry to the mediaeval settlers of Goathland.

The story of Goathland emerges from the stories of four separate communities which by 1517 have become so interlinked as to be one. Beckhole is different; it is both part of the story and a story on its own. The book reflects this and Beckhole's tale is told in a separate section.

No community stands still and the author's experience in the first half of the 20th century add the final brush strokes to this evocative picture of a moorland community.

the Pickering parish, this caused considerable difficulties. Finally, the King issued a special writ to deal with the situation: 'the church of Pickering shall have the parish which it had in King Edward's time, notwithstanding the erection of any new chapels and shall have the tithes also.'

From that time the various abbots of Whitby developed the farm as a grange of the abbey but the chapel was priested from Pickering.

As time went on the Brothers became widely known. A *toft* in Lockton was given to them by William Boie about 1150. This is the first mention of their chapel by name — *St. Mary at Godeland*. With various repairs, a new thatch and stalls in 1594, the addition of one or two windows in 1661, the chapel survived until 1821 when it appears to have been unsafe. The old stone altar and a pulpit from the ancient church are preserved in the present church which was built in 1892.

In 1206 a fourth charter shows that the Abbot paid King John 100 shillings and gave him a white palfrey in order to retain *Godeland Hermitage*. Between this date and the forest Eyre Court held from 1334 to 1338 further progress, particularly in stock rearing, took place. There are indications that the land had been divided and let to two tenants, with a third portion worked for the abbey itself.

In 1334 the Abbot was accused of turning out more stock upon the common than he had any right to do. They said he was allowed twenty cows and a bull but he overstocked by ten cows. He was summoned to answer in the *Eyre Court*. At this time the abbey at Whitby was at the height of its grandeur. The Abbot attended the Court in person, at Pickering. He was an authoritative, rich and powerful man, producing his charter which showed unlimited pasturage throughout the King's Pickering pasturage. The foresters were irritated at their failure and only waited a year or so before they tried to convict him once more.

This time the Abbot refused to go to Pickering again and said it was the duty of the Justices to come within his *Liberty of Whitby* to hear and determine any pleas against him. The Justices allowed his claim and arranged a Court at Hackness. They bade him attend in person, bringing with him 'his men', that is, those who were cultivating the arable land and looking after the stock at the Hermitage for the benefit of the abbey, and 'his tenants', which is interesting because it shows that in 1336 part of the land was already let. Since it says tenants there must have been at least two of them.

The Abbot held all the cards as he had done before but his behaviour led to an enmity in *Godeland* which must have been very uncomfortable for both his men and his tenants.

Godeland had now developed into a straggling village partially cleared and enclosed though there was much scrub and forest land still surrounding it. A few houses were built near the little chapel and the priest from the Hermitage had a small congregation. It is probable that he cultivated the field known as Chapel Hill, in lieu of the glebe land usually attached to larger churches.

The Hermitage building had decayed through the years. In 1494 Abbot William Colsen decided to repair or rebuild, perhaps both, as he used the right given in the charters of 1100 to apply to Sir Brian Sandford, steward of the Duchy of Lancaster at Pickering for oaks from the forest as *housebote*. Thirty-six such trees were forthcoming. They were used for three pairs of crucks or forks, beams and wall plates for a new house of two bays, possibly about 30 ft. long and one storey high. The simplest possible construction for the building would have been used. The problem of providing for man, cattle and stores under the same roof perhaps means that the old building was restored also. It seems that the new buildings were still used as a grange of the abbey until the shadow of Dissolution loomed nearer.

In 1538 Abbot Henry de Vall, the last man to be Abbot of Whitby, leased the house, now called Abbot's House, and land to Robert Cockerill, a Goathland farmer, for 81 years at an annual rent of 20 shillings. However, when on 14th December 1539 the abbey was surrendered, the lease of this house and farm became null and void. When Robert Cockerill signed his lease it could never have crossed his mind that the name of a humble farmer would be for ever associated with the last Abbot of Whitby, and that his little farm would be worked prosperously, four hundred years later, when the magnificent abbey was a roofless ruin on its cliff overlooking the sea.

Later the house and land were sold to Robert Bushell. Richard Bushell inherited but in 1617 he sold it to Nicholas Bushell, a well known Whitby merchant and ship-owner who in 1631 sold it once more. Two *tenements* are given as part of the land in Goathland, Abbot's House and Thorneley Farm.

Since the time of the Dissolution an old tradition surrounding the Brothers' Hermitage has passed down the years, springing no doubt from the ancient charters. Each new owner seems to have been required for his well-being and good fortune to blow a horn on Sill Howe. This is a shadow remaining from requirements of the charters to entertain poor travellers and attract them to where there was lodging and food. It appears to have been observed once at least when any new owner took over, until this century, but it is now obsolete.

The hospitality of the Hermitage ceased at the Dissolution. Since the main road between Whitby and Pickering then passed its door, a little inn called the *Wayside Inn* was built, which also served the small surrounding community. It is thought that George Sleightholme was the licensee here in 1615 and William Prust was recorded as the innkeeper in the church register of 1725.

In 1619 the property was in the hands of Nicholas Bushell who headed the Court on a survey of Goathland undertaken for the Duchy of Lancaster by John Norden. In 1698 the Bushell family name ceased with the death of Robert Bushell. Hereafter Abbot's House was in the hands of Thomas Williamson, a haberdasher of London, and Elinor his wife, who decided to sell it in 1707.

From the time of this sale to Isabel Craven of Sinnington, a widow who had formerly been the wife of William Dove of Goathland, the deeds exist.

In 1740 the Craven family sold it to William Mintoft a Goathland weaver, the house being rebuilt in 1743 upon the old site.

In 1779 Peter Harwood, a farmer from Hunmanby, bought the land. He rebuilt the house but retained the Mintoft date stone. In 1927, four generations later, the last of the Harwoods died and the property was sold.

There is little else to tell. The old inn has gone and the main road between Whitby and Pickering now runs over the moor via Eller Beck. The way of the ancient turf road is almost obliterated. The ford where carts crossed the beck is still there but the pack horse bridge is no more, though in the water below the present crossing its foundations can be seen.

Abbot's Lane, deep sunken by centuries of traffic was almost destroyed in 1934 by a flood, since when the Council has never repaired it. Two stone way markers remain but the old wooden signpost to Pickering, which stood well into this century, rotted away and heather now covers the site.

Thorneley Farm was last mentioned when the North Eastern Railway bought some land at Abbot's House in 1863 but it has been pulled down. Any land it had is amalgamated with Abbot's House.

WHEELDALE AND HUNT HOUSE

heeldale is about 1500 acres of high moorland south of the parish of Egton, taking its name from the wheel-like conformation of the beck of that name. It was within the *Regard of Pickering Forest*, and in parts was heavily wooded, but as no timber could be felled lawfully in such a wood, it had no worth as income to anyone. The *Regard*, composed of twelve or more knights, inspected it in theory every three years, answering questions required of them, noting where enclosures had been made on the waste, whether by warrant or not, or where encroachments for houses had occurred.

The earliest story concerning Wheeldale is of Peter de Mauley who became a ward of King Henry III in 1241 when his father Peter I, the Lord of Egton and Mulgrave died. His estates stretched out over the Egton moor until they reached the wood and moor of Wheeldale where, in 1251, it appears he was using 40 acres of the King's *demesne* and claiming it as his own. When the King demanded the land, Peter rendered it up as the King's right but at the same time petitioned that it should be granted in *fee-farm* to him, i.e. a perpetual rent of about a quarter of the true value.

Geoffrey de Langele, Justice of the King's Forest, was instructed about the annual value of the wood and moor. By a further writ, he was commanded to find out if it would be to the King's loss to grant this in *fee-farm* to Peter.

An enquiry was made at Pickering and the boundaries of the King's *demesne* and forest in Wheeldale were set out. The Jury suggested 'it would be to the King's advantage to let Peter have the entire area for 10 marks per year in fee-farm so that the wood and moor remain the Forest of the King and within the Regard as it always had been.' (A mark in medieval times was worth 13s.4d.). In this way a check could be kept on the tenant.

In the above enquiry the name of *Hunterhuses* is mentioned. Possibly it

Hunt House

may not apply only to the present site of Hunt House but to a small district lying between the modern Blawath and Wardlerigg.

Whether a farm occupied the present site of Hunt House in 1251 when the enquiry was held or whether it came into being during the next fifty years is not known, but in 1301 the 'Lay Subsidy for Goyelaunde' shows that Thoma del Hontehous paid 2s.10¾d.

When Thomas Ughtred was Constable of Pickering Castle, the Ministers Accounts of 1322 tell that Thoma del Hontehous rented a *messuage* with meadow and pasture at Wheeldale for 13s.11d.

A wood in the wilds of Wheeldale was a continual temptation to unlawful felling, for fuel was a necessity. Anyone using waggons to take timber out of the *demesne* woods not only incurred a fine in proportion to the value of the timber but if the offence was repeated, forfeited the waggon and team. Many people from Egton and Goathland were presented at the *Eyre Court* of 1334 for cutting down oaks from Wheeldale.

The removal of these trees ultimately left much small top and branch wood. In 1322 Robert Short, a smith, applied for:

1. A licence to work a forge in Wheeldale for which he paid 5 shillings.
2. A place where he could make a charcoal factory, and the purchase of dry wood for this which cost 13s 11d.
3. A licence to live in Wheeldale which warrant must be shown to the Regarders on demand.

The names and dwelling places of all tenants in 1572 are known from an agreement whereby the Duchy granted a lease of Goathland to Maurice Barkley.

Mary Hardinge, Gentlewoman, paid a *fee-farm* rent of 15 shillings. This lady proved to be a relative of the Ratcliffes of Ugthorpe Hall, the owner of which, Roger Ratcliffe, appears to have later purchased the house and lands. In his will made in 1588 he granted to his eldest daughter Katheryn Ratcliffe 'all those my farms and Tenementes of Hunthouse and Wheildaile with the appurtenances, Scituat, Lieing and beinge in the Countie of Yorke.'

The Hardinges and Ratcliffes were important Roman Catholic families. Hunt House became a refuge for those being persecuted for abiding by the old religion in a country now professedly Protestant. They took many poor folk into their employ. Two of these, James and Dorothie Crossbye, were presented in the year 1595 by the Goathland Churchwardens, Robert Harland and Randulph Skinner, at the Ecclesiastical Court of the Dean of York for not coming to church and for not receiving Holy Communion. After being so presented for several years they were, in 1600, declared to be Roman Catholic and servants of Mistress Katheryn Ratcliffe (who had herself been in gaol in 1593 for practising as a Roman Catholic). Until 1614, they escaped the Court of Quarter Sessions but when both aged 63 had to answer at Helmsley along with other Goathland people.

When Mistress Katheryn Ratcliffe of Ugthorpe made her will on 31st January 1614 she left to Dorothie Crosbie 'two kye gates, food for two cows, (apparently at Hunt House) winter and summer during her life.' All her servants were given small sums of money and other things. Among these beneficiaries is the name of Christopher Simpson, one of several men of that name to be associated with Hunt House. He was left 20 shillings. By trade he was a master shoemaker but warrants were out for his apprehension as 'an obstinate convicted popishe recusant hiding himself so as law cannot be executed against him.' From other sources it is known that he wandered the country playing in *Interludes* but it seems he may by 1614 have settled with his wife and son, another Christopher Simpson, at Hunt House, which Katheryn Ratcliffe had bequeathed to Railph Hardinge.

The story of the Simpsons of Hunt House continues about 130 years and five generations of men with the same Christian name. Christopher and Dorothy Simpson married in 1604 and had 5 children — Christopher, Stephen, Thomas, William and Eleanor, who it seems were brought up at Hunt House where their father may have taken the place of James Crosbie, in the employ after 1614 of Railph Hardinge.

There is no corroborative evidence that the Simpsons were at Hunt House until the Duchy leased its intakes in Goathland to Sir John Watson and Sir James Fullerton on 10th July 1627. The list of holders was published in January 1628. A Christopher Simpson held a 3 acre intake at Hunt House for 5 shillings per annum. He appears again in the Commonwealth Report of 1651 when the rent is raised to 12 shillings on improvement.

In 1628 the young Christopher would be about 22 or 25 years old, helping his father on the farm. He had become passionately fond of music, perhaps fostered by inmates who were hiding in the house and had discovered the young man's talent. Through the Justices order for Roman Catholics,

The Plough Stots

A reminder of Goathland's Norse origins.

movement was curtailed to a limit of five miles. In the isolation of this remote moorland, music must have been a consolation.

When Charles I declared open war he gave command of the four northern counties of England to William Cavendish, Duke of Newcastle. It is known that the second Christopher Simpson left home and joined the Duke of Newcastle's Army as in the 2nd edition of his *Compendium of Music* he says he served with the Duke's army in the Civil War.

The battle of Marston Moor occurred on the 1st July 1644, and with the defeat of the Royalists there, Newcastle fled abroad from Scarborough and the hold on the County collapsed. The sufferings of the fleeing Royalists were great but some time later Christopher Simpson came to Scampton in Lincolnshire. Here he visited Sir Robert Bolles with whom he may have come into contact in 1643 when Newcastle's forces were in Lincolnshire. Sir Robert, a confirmed Royalist himself became his Patron, made him Music Tutor to his sons and maintained him in his home until his death. During Sir Robert's life Simpson published the book *The Division Viol* which he dedicated to him; later when the second edition referred to above was published he dedicated it to his old pupil, by then Sir John Bolles.

After Christopher (2) left home, his brother Stephen's son also Christopher (3) came to take his place at Hunt House and was working there in 1663 when the musician bought it, presumably from the Hardinges. Why he did this is not apparent, but there seems to have been some pressure, because practically all his assets and the money from his publications was spent on acquiring it. He made his will on 5th May 1669 and settled Hunt House upon his nephew, with the farm land, but the terms of the will show his poverty.

The previous year, 24th January 1668, Christopherus Simpson (3) et Martha Harrison, Nupt. is entered in the Register of Egton Church. Possibly they rebuilt part of Hunt House as the lettering above the old door (now inside the building) is C.S.M. 1685.

He and Martha brought up their family there, but all was not well, for on 25th September 1695 he and his son, Christopher (4) now a man of about twenty-six years granted a lease of Hunt House for 1000 years to the use of George Hobson of Horsebridge, Durham, and Frances Pearson of Harestones (called Haystones today).

Whether this need for money was due to fines as Roman Catholics or some other reason cannot be seen today, but Christopher (4) was married during the following year, their subsequent children being baptised at Goathland Church. Yet in 1717 under 'Registration of Papist Estates' all their Goathland property was registered.

Both holders of the Hunt House lease were dead by 1738 and an Indenture made in that year assigns Hunt House and farm to Joseph Oxley of Glaisdale for the residue of the term. In May 1742 the Simpsons granted him the freehold in return for cancellation of debts and an extra £87.2s.0d.

Joseph Oxley with his daughter Ann married to Andrew Cook of Hart Hall, Glaisdale, came to Hunt House permanently in 1748. Several children were registered in the Baptismal Register of Goathland including Joseph, the eldest, born 9th February 1748.

In 1778 the grandfather died leaving the farm to his grandson, Joseph. He with his wife Elizabeth (Dale) were living there and a daughter, Ann, was baptised at Goathland. It seems they moved into the Middleton-Aislaby district about 1797, letting the farm to Joseph Ward, but they still retained an interest in Goathland giving a donation toward the erection of a school in 1808. In 1813 when old people who knew Goathland were called to give evidence about the rightful boundary of Allan Tofts, Joseph Cook then aged 65 did so at York Assizes.

About 1815 the Hill family built a shooting lodge on an intake near the farm which it seems they had previously bought, and called in Hunt Hall. In 1907 both these houses were sold.

In 1812 Thomas and Mary Smith were tenants of Hunt House where their daughter Susannah and sons John, William and James were born. All the boys worked on the farm, James being particularly interested in shepherding. It was a good flock and later when William, known throughout the district as Willy, took over from his father, the farm became noted for its prize rams and Scots Blackface Sheep. At one time he was Hon. Treasurer to the Black-Face Breeders' Association. He was also Master of Hounds for the trencher fed Goathland pack for over a quarter of a century. William was churchwarden for nearly half a century. He rode his horse to church, stabling it in the parish stable near *Cross Pipes Inn*, but his sheep dog accompanied him into church, lying quietly beneath his pew. He married rather late in life. His son John was born in 1866 and his daughter Elizabeth in 1867. He died in 1914 aged 92 years.

The last house to be occupied in Wheeldale, and probably the only one to be built there since that of Robert Short, smith, in the 14th century, was one in which lived William Pinkney who farmed a few acres still known as Pinkney's Intakes.

Today Wheeldale is well known, and hundreds of people come to it every summer to see the Roman Road which runs over it. This was uncovered by James Patterson, keeper to the Duchy of Lancaster, about 1912. The Keeper's House in the Valley is a Youth Hostel, and Hunt Hall a private house. With the excellent road into Goathland, Wheeldale is no longer isolated or remote.

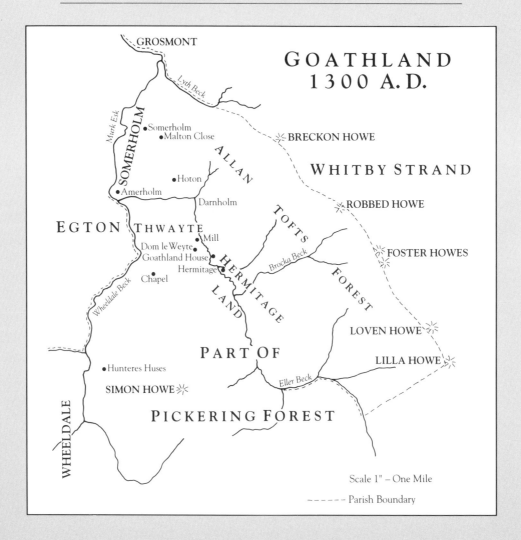

GOATHLAND
1300 A.D.

GROSMONT

Lyth Beck

Mark Esk

SOMERHOLM

Somerholm
Malton Close

BRECKON HOWE

WHITBY STRAND

ALLAN

Hoton

Amerholm

Darnholm

ROBBED HOWE

EGTON THWAYTE

TOFTS

Dom le Weyte
Goathland House
Hermitage

Mill

Brocka Beck

FOSTER HOWES

FOREST

HERMITAGE

Chapel

Wheeldale Beck

LAND

LOVEN HOWE

LILLA HOWE

PART OF

Hunteres Huses

Eller Beck

SIMON HOWE

WHEELDALE

PICKERING FOREST

Scale 1" – One Mile

- - - - - Parish Boundary

SETTLERS ON ALLAN TOFTS

oday, clad with heather and bracken, Allan Tofts (Allen's enclosures) rises gently to a height of over 900 ft. on its eastern boundary.

When recorded history began 800 years ago the horizon must have appeared much as it does now, crowned by the burial places locally called *howes*, erected by Bronze Age man 3000 years earlier. But before that time Allan Tofts had no name. It was merely the extreme northern end of the king's great forest of Pickering: twisted wind blown oaks, grey ashes, underwood of thorn, holly and hazel, and coverts of rough grass among briars and brambles, where red and fallow deer lived.

Below Lilla Howe where, in 626, Lilla, counsellor of King Edwin of Northumbria, was interred, rises the Eller Beck. This little stream was Allan Tofts boundary to Beckhole, after which, joining the West Beck, the river is known as the Murk Esk until it joins the Esk at Grosmont. The boundary turned sharply up the steep Lyth Beck valley on to the moor where, still climbing, now under the lonely sky, it reached the *howes* again. There was then no connection with any land on the west of the river.

The first reliable information comes from the *Pipe Rolls* of 1165. Then, it seems that the forest of Scalby near to Scarborough, Langdale and what was later to become Allan Tofts were accounted together for fiscal purposes. Before 1200 two foresters Alan de Thornton and Alan de Boie are known, the latter accounting (several years running) for £2 from the three places. One of them may have been responsible for making and letting small holdings so giving his name to the *tofts*, first called Allan Tofts in 1204.

On 30th June 1267, Henry III gave his younger son Edmund Plantagenet the Manor, forest and castle of Pickering, with the manor of Scalby. This gift included Allan Tofts. As part of his bailiwick the forester-in-fee for Pickering and Scalby, Roger Bigod had certain benefits of the job. When servants of the new owner began to cut down trees he claimed the stripped bark and branches as his, which led to quarrels.

Lord Edmund's servants were instructed to clear some of the forest land and turn it into farms. Trees, thickets and coverts were rooted up. This action was called *assarting* land. To do it without licence was a grave offence against Forest Laws, but the servants had Letters Patent to protect them and by order of the bailiff Robert Conescliff, something like 190 acres were *assarted*, or encroached, and enclosed, rents being fixed for their use.

Many names still in existence tell a little of the history: green and thwaite mean a clearing, Green End marks the end of the clearing.

This had all taken a considerable time but now that the new tenants were established on their holdings another complaint came from the forester-in-fee that because of the enclosure he was deprived of pasture. His bailiff, Peter de Molington, as a gesture of defiance, or so it seems, made an encroachment in a place called Somerholm, a long sunny hillside sloping down to the Murk Esk, built a house there and let the farm for 10 shillings a year. He appears to have got away with this piece of impudence, for being called upon to answer for it in the *Eyre Court* of 1282, it was discovered he had received rent for nine years.

A later Lancaster bailiff caused another 300 acres to be encroached. This means that around 500 acres were taken for agricultural land, which plus a few scattered intakes of the 16th century agrees very well with the amount of land used there today.

The largest holding belonged to Malton Priory, the 91 acre farm now known as Morton Close. As the Priory derived two thirds of its income from wool this *grange* would rent a large sheep stray. It has been suggested that a stone wall stretching from above Malton Close towards Hawthorn Hill ending at the top of Water Ark Scar enclosed a sheep stray of theirs. Less than a hundred years ago it was called 'The Crag'. It then stood two feet high according to old folks' testimony, but being used as a quarry for sheep bields and field walls only a thin line of stone now remains.

The land at Hawthorn Hill was possibly a Norse or Danish development as a carved monolith found there indicates, and was cultivated long before Lord Edmund's time. Its name was Houghton in 1600, supposedly derived from the Norse *hoton* meaning 'farm on the hill'. Altogether about twenty places were let in Allan Tofts, but besides this were hundreds of acres of waste heavily wooded in parts, particularly towards the south.

Allan Tofts foresters were appointed by deed and served for life, the wages received being 20 shillings for a coat, probably a distinctive uniform, and five quarters of wheat a year. No-one had the right to cut down any living wood either on the waste or in their holdings. They did so if necessary — mostly small saplings springing from the boles of timber trees previously felled. For this they paid a small fine for *vert* — the right to fell.

The most famous account is that of the Prior of Malton who, having to provide his Canons with kippers for winter eating, thought nothing could be handier than to clear some of the thorn and hazel from Malton Close, to smoke them. He bought his supply of herrings from Scarborough cobles to have them kippered in the fish house there. But alas! As the waggons left Malton Close he was discovered moving 'green hue of thorn and hazel' and was summoned to answer for this and fined £5.

Allan Tofts was included in the list of the 'King's Ageastments'. Animals pasturing there must be branded with the special mark +. In early times there was no right of pasture there without payment and an *agister* enforced these small sums.

Around Michaelmas each year a forest drift was made. Such cattle as had strayed into Allan Tofts, being unbranded, were seized. Their owners were fined in the *Swainmote Court*, the cattle being recovered only when their full value was received.

Allan Tofts tenants and others fared very badly during the second decade of the 14th century. There was a run of bad weather, poor harvests and lean years. Many families failed to survive, their holdings too small to support them in such circumstances. Farms were deserted, rentals dropped, many places were recorded in the Ministers Accounts as 'decayed'.

These people lived in houses of one or two rooms, crowded by the family and shared with the animals. The rooms were windowless, earth floored with a fire of sorts upon the floor. Beds were of bracken and black bread and oatmeal porridge were for food.

So the first attempt to colonise Allan Tofts came to a standstill; the reason given is 'the land is unoccupied on account of the poverty of the country.' Of these tenants there is little information, just a name, Thomas Reed, with his 2½ acres, or a story such as that of the Prior with his kippers. The others, occupying the rest of the land, remain unknown.

The land was occupied again around the second half of the 15th century, Allan Tofts and Goathland becoming one village with a combined rental of £21.8s.4d.

In 1572 a rent roll shows as many tenants on Allan Tofts as in Goathland. Malton Close is no longer a *grange* but divided equally between two tenants sharing house and land.

In 1542 Sir Richard Cholmley took a lease of Goathland and Allan Tofts, ordering all the tenants to enclose pieces of the waste. These he let for a small yearly rent and collected a fine on occupation, to the great annoyance of the farmers. Some pieces were used as arable, allowing the old worn out corn land to rest, some were pasture, which provided for an extra cow, while those that were meadow gave winter feed, a commodity always in short supply.

Many of these intakes can be identified, the block for three farms and Bank House, twelve acres, equally divided, still stands in isolation on the moor, all used by the one occupant of the Hawthorn Hill land today and known as 't'Oughteron Close' by the last generation.

On the rental of a lease in 1572 there are twelve or thirteen holdings of various sizes on Allan Tofts, four of them very small.

Timber had been getting scarcer as years went by, sold, stolen or taken by various Duchy stewards for their own use, or allotted as *housebote*, yet when a survey of woods was made during Elizabethan times, Malton Close still had 300 timber oaks growing on its land, i.e. trees which at 6 ft. above the stump were a foot square, as well as hundreds of scrub oaks. A nearby farm, Southe House, had a bank sloping down into the valley with 5 acres of timber oak and ash, so despite the depredations there was much more woodland left than one would suppose, since the same applies to most of the holdings.

By the 17th century, people had begun to live more secure and comfortable lives, though the climate was the same as ever. In 1657 Allantoft Farm belonged to Philip Addison and his wife, Christian. The house was thatched with two rooms and by this time there were cow houses and barns for its stock. Inside, its inmates had cushions on the settle and buffet stools, beds of chaff or feathers, with pillows, and pewter plates were taking the place of the wooden plates (doublers). When Philip died he left his wife and his son John equal shares of the 'Free Lands', which were all

Always a Warm Welcome

Hawthorn Hill, childhood home of the author.

to become John's on his mother's death. There were younger children in the family, and in the father's will he touchingly marked out for John, on whom now devolved the responsibility of providing a living for them, 'two black oxen calves known as Jewel and Wanton, and a bay mare' for his own.

Hawthorne Hill, of which the Sleightholmes took the tenancy towards the end of the 1600s, was smaller. In 1697 Elizabeth Sleightholme, a widow, died there, leaving her son William and daughter Elizabeth, the older children, to manage the farm and bring up two younger girls and a boy. The house was of the usual pattern, a forehouse or living room, in this case containing a bed as well as a table, three stools and three chairs, with the parlour used as a bedroom next to it. This had two beds, chests with linen, a chair and three spinning wheels. Under the thatch was a space called the chamber, containing two stones of wool and some implements.

The farm animals were two oxen for ploughing, two cows, three heffers, one stirk, two stears, with one 'old horse with its furnitory'. On the moor were forty sheep and forty lambs.

Five pounds worth of hay and corn were stored, but as Elizabeth died in August, though the hay would have been gathered, the year's corn supply would still have been standing in the fields.

The houses had *turbary* rights and could therefore cut peat and turf for fuel. During the 18th century thin seams of coal were discovered in several places, above Water Ark, in Bradley and Mill Woods, and at Darnholm. This was obtained by opencast working or from drifts in the hillsides. No doubt some of it was used in the houses but it was only of poor quality, its chief use being in lime kilns. Trains of pack donkeys transported it to Pickering bringing back lime for use on the land.

Sandstone was quarried in several places being much in demand for stone sleepers, buildings, and foundations of the wooden bridges constructed during the making of the horse-drawn railway line of 1836 between Whitby and Pickering.

Later the great intrusion of volcanic rock at Sill Howe was quarried for road metal, the Duchy of Lancaster leasing the right to Messrs. Melrose and Bradley of York. They also allowed, with the consent of the common right holders, a tramway to be built for transporting the stone. After the Second World War these works were closed and the waste resulting from former operations removed for use in road making.

The story of the 'Disputed Moor', involving an enquiry into the boundary of Allan Tofts in 1812, was first told me by an elderly man of Green End. Later a report of the proceedings was discovered in the Parish Chest. The boundary was from Lyth Beck head to Brockrigg head, the dispute really being about sheep pasture. It finally became so heated that the Lord of the Manor of Sleights brought an action against the Lord of the Manor of Goathland which was heard at York Assizes on 15th March 1813.

Three interesting things arose from this action:

1. Testimony on behalf of the correct boundary was given by ancient inhabitants, some resident, some retired, three of them over 80 years of age. The true boundary was determined and judgement was given for Goathland.
2. During the hearing, part of the boundary is described as 'crossing the Turnpike and persuing the direction of the old road on the East Side of the Turnpike, and what was used as the ancient Road before the Turnpike Road was made.'
3. When the result was made known the Goathland Overseers made haste to employ the village stone mason to renew the 'Bounder Stones' on the Disputed Boundary.

One of these stones backing on to the Sneaton Boundary Stone bears the inscription 'Goathland Boundary determined at York Assizes 1813' and is standing now.

Today's farms — Hollin Garth, Liberty Hall and Green End Farm work all Somerholm between them, while Morton Close, Dale End (probably the old Crag Cliff) and Greenland (once Long Close) cultivate the remainder of the land of that area. All the land at Hawthorn Hill including the Intakes and Bradley is worked together, the farm house standing where the ancient *hoton* once stood.

DEVELOPMENT OF THWAYTE

After the development of Allan Tofts Lord Edmund's steward built a mill upon the Eller Beck to grind the corn of the new tenants. Since that time until the beginning of the 20th century a corn mill has occupied the site. Today, no longer needed for its original purpose it has been altered inside to make a delightful cottage.

The steward then turned to the land at the west side of the beck called Thwayte. The area was flat. A few trees grew upon it but it was mostly bush, scrub, briars, blackberries and coarse grass. A few squatters by hard work had reclaimed an acre or two of portions of this flattish land. They had improved it little by little, sufficiently to turn it into arable. Among them may have been one or two working with permission but the others, when discovered were fined on the grounds that the deer were disturbed and their sustenance threatened. They were then allowed to retain their holdings for a small sum annually. The names of a few early settlers are recorded. Ada Prudhomme, John le Styrkehyrd, Elena Brocedyff, Johanne de Lindrygg, John son of Robert, with others.

Such crops as they grew must have been meagre, providing the most frugal of livings. As far as one can discover any record, wheat and rye appear to have been broadcast in the autumn, harvested and then ground together for the meal called maslin from which coarse brown bread was baked. The spring sowings were oats, pulses and barley.

The only real development was in the vicinity of the Hermitage. For nearly 200 years various abbots of Whitby had cleared trees and scrub bringing their *carucate* under the plough. By right of their charters, sheep and cattle fed on the forest waste. Upon Little Beck which ran through their land was built a sheep fold for safety during the night. Sometime later the Hermitage land appears to have been let as separate farms.

Few things are known for certain about the great forest on the Hermitage land. The charters indicate that there were foresters caring for it who delivered timber for their *housebote* and *hedge-bote* and who had specific instructions not to interfere with the Brothers' farming or their animals. As for the Brothers themselves they were respected in the countryside, being well known in the villages of Lockton and Levisham, and in the town of Pickering.

In 1267 when Henry III gave Pickering Forest to his son Edmund, the intention was that it should be used as a free chase. However, in 1285 Edmund prevailed on his brother, now the king, to grant him the privilege of having his own Justices appointed for the forest, receiving the fines for himself. This meant that the whole force of Forest Law appertained in Pickering as it did in Royal forests. Many transgressions are reported, some involving Goathland men, but the chief prosecutions were for deer hunting and stealing. As a rule the principal culprits were men of position who were heavily fined. Their beaters and servants mostly had no financial assets and were frequently outlawed, and their goods forfeited — a calamity which fell upon more than one Goathland tenant.

The Abbot of Whitby had common pasture over all the land, but this could be partly set aside provided enough remained for necessary pasture. On the west side of the Eller Beck, at Thwayte, the land was mostly clay, not leaf mould and peat like Allan Tofts, needing good ploughs to cultivate it with success. A great eight oxen plough was used to render this old forest ground fit to let as arable farm land. The names Thwaitefield, Waitekits and Wheathill together with the High Twates and Low Twates of the 19th century still remain.

On the west edge of the improved area two pasture fields called East and West Common Fields were enclosed, possibly for the use of young stock, should the Abbot change his mind about the new tenants' use of the common grazing.

Common pasture was vital to these people with small arable holdings — the animals they acquired had to be kept in good condition.

In 1251, before Pickering was bestowed on Lord Edmund, an enquiry had been made as to 'what men of the King's demesne were wont to have in the forest.' There it is set out that they were to have common pasture for all animals except goats, with acorns for their pigs.

Other necessary and useful things were also provided for in the enquiry.

Foresters would deliver both green and dead wood for building or repairs to the *tenements*, with wood for hedges and the making of ploughs, tools and household utensils. Their firewood they could gather for themselves from the small sticks always lying under the trees, or by pulling dead boughs reached by hook or crook from the trees themselves.

These concessions were necessary and useful, but it is clearly set out that at this early period the tenants enjoyed these amenities as a privilege, solely by sufferance of the bailiffs and by the goodwill of the king and not of right.

Edward I harassed by raids of the Scots upon the northern counties whose destroying, robbing, murdering sorties penetrated as far south as Pickering, levied a tax in 1301 to pay for the war. It was one-fifteenth of every person's moveable goods, and nobody was exempt.

This return still exists in its complete form for the villages around Goathland, for Pickering, of which the growing Goathland was a township, and for Goathland itself. It reveals a good deal about the new developments, as Goathland and Allan Tofts are included together. Even with the Prior of Malton and the Abbot of Whitby both of whom had farm establishments, there were only fifteen names on the list, the complete sum gathered being £1.17s.5¾d.

This Lay Subsidy as it is known, is a silent witness of the poverty of Goathland's first settlers, but some of them struggled on with their only help, the soil. They had but crude tools and simple methods of cultivation to provide all that they, their households and animals needed, so obviously the seven or eight acre holdings could only sustain a limited number of people.

Their isolation was almost complete, nothing was obtained except by their own continual effort.

Pause a moment to consider. From sunrise to sunset they worked on the holdings. The corn they grew provided all the bread they had, no nipping down to the shop when flour ran out. In any season the months before the new harvest was ready were months of hunger and weakness, in bad seasons starvation.

Remember too, need for new clothing meant the sheep must be bred and clipped, the wool scoured, teased, spun, dyed and woven into cloth, which then must be cut and sewn by themselves.

There was no tradesman's name on the Lay Subsidy Roll, but after about twenty years a blacksmith set up a forge in Wheeldale. He smelted his iron with charcoal, so had to procure a licence from the forest authorities to use 'dry wood' from Wheeldale.

Some years ago a primitive iron smelting furnace (now in Whitby Museum) was found on the moor above Goathland Church, not far from the thin seam of iron worked at Killing Pits. It is dated 14th century.

The land here was held according to the custom of the manor and 'at the will' of the lord. On a dangerous limestone cliff in Newton Dale, called Killing Noble Scarr, nested the peregrine falcon, a powerful hawk used for bird hunting. It could only be captured as it left its breeding places, so the tenure of the Goathland inhabitants was to watch it for the King's use. This was an easy tenure and appears to be the only one, and from what can be learnt it appears one or two of the leading farmers did the work having as a reward one or two closes under the Scarr.

During evidence given by Goathland men to a Commission in 1612 enquiring about the boundaries, George Cockerill speaking says 'and there hath been Hawkes bred in Newton Dale in Killingnoble Scarr which the Inhabitants of Goathland was charged to watch for the King's use ...'. William Keld who was older than George takes the story back into the early 1500s and says this was so, and that his Father had two folds under Killingnoble Scarr within the said bounds, one for Swine and another for Horse.

Goathland peasants found their freedom curtailed in several ways. They could take little except firewood from the forest to help them survive. Foresters made demands upon them, and every year the king asked for a few of their sparse coins. This *tallage* is recorded for a curious reason. Henry VII needed money for Scottish wars, for the marauding Scots were still a plague on the northern counties.

Among all the tenants here was one freeman and the account tells us that:

> 'the said Sir Roger Hastings holds at Will of the King a Fermehold in Gottland wher uppon he keps XXxx (400)shepe and iijxx (60) Catall for which the Constable and Inhabitants there taxed hys said Catall and shepe as they dyd there awn, and what tyme as the Constable come to axe the said taxe he answered theme that he was not the kinges bound, he was fre born and none shuld have of hym...'

Naturally the Constable and inhabitants complained. Here was a man with probably more stock than the peasants had altogether. Why shouldn't he pay too?

In this case however the *tallage* would be of benefit to the whole community freeing them from the Scottish raids, and free men were liable too. Sir Roger finally paid the tax in 1499.

When those in high places set bad examples to their fellows, others follow suit. The Wars of the Roses created difficult times in Pickering Forest. Crown property was wasted and destroyed by the very people who should have preserved it. Inhabitants of the forest and others living on the verges saw this lawlessness. There were few officers left to say anything to them, so the trees were cut, game, even deer taken, *assarts* made without permission and though Henry VII appointed new officers and made stricter rules the era of freedom had been tasted.

––––––––––––

The 15th century came to an end with the general pattern of Goathland houses and farmland set. This remained until the middle of the 19th century, when the old village with its self-contained economy began to pass away. The names of the occupiers endured through many generations, a few of them to the present day.

All worked with unremitting toil to keep starvation at bay, but pastures and meadows which are never fertilised, eaten and mowed every year without ceasing, became unprofitable, for naturally having all food to provide made the farmer put his corn and pulse before the hay for the stock. His manure, more precious than we can imagine today, went to fertilise the arable land, but there was very little even for this. Winter feed was too often in short supply even to keep the breeding stock going. Animals were reduced to a minimum, salted down or smoked for winter food. Even so belts were generally tightened before the next harvest could be gathered.

During the 15th century the Duchy stepped in to help tenants in a practical fashion which remains to this day. As the old forest had diminished, although many woodlands still remained, coarse grass, herbage and scrub grew up suitable for oxen, cattle and sheep pasture. Portions were granted through the Manor Court, and were known as the Lez Feld Stakes, which interpreted is unenclosed grazing rights in the open country. This free range feeding supplemented their own poor pastures, and though a flock of sheep took time to build up, it gave hope of easement, with, in the future wool making money. Altogether sheep held much worth, they were always productive, giving milk from which cheese could be made, lambs, wool, and moreover unlike the cattle, could get a living in winter as well as summer and do reasonably well even on poor grass.

TUDOR TIMES

The Customary tenants of Goathland left the Manor Court of April 1518 in twos and threes exchanging their bits of gossip before ways parted and they took the undulating tracks to their homes having performed their service for another six months.

There were no stone causeways, no hard roads; these came later. A grassy loning led to Beckhole. For the rest, well defined paths trodden by friends and neighbours linked up the irregularly spaced houses. Except to church and mill there was no great amount of traffic. Of the holdings little could be discerned, their heather thatched roofs so blending into the earth that they were one with it, hummocks sprinkled over the moor. Only rising smoke with its sweet smell of burning wood and turf betrayed them.

Farming in 1518 was the same as it had been in their fathers' times. It was still mere subsistence farming, a surplus only when weather allowed a good year. The threat of hunger was commonplace to these people.

There were superficial changes which had begun when the Duchy of Lancaster bestowed the right of the Lez Feld Stakes, but in the early 16th century the advantages were putting little into the farmers' pockets, and their old traditional way of life had not altered.

The outlying farms of Goathland today, Greenlands on the north-east and Hunthouse on the south-west, are the same as they were in Tudor times. The other holdings, some poor and small, none large, were scattered between them, over the 15,000 acres of the township. In these the peasant community lived. Women probably never left the village between birth and death and the men rarely. The total population was about 110.

If a market were needed, Egton, only five miles distant, was comparatively easy of access, but Whitby twice as far, had no road to it and could not easily be approached unless the weather was good.

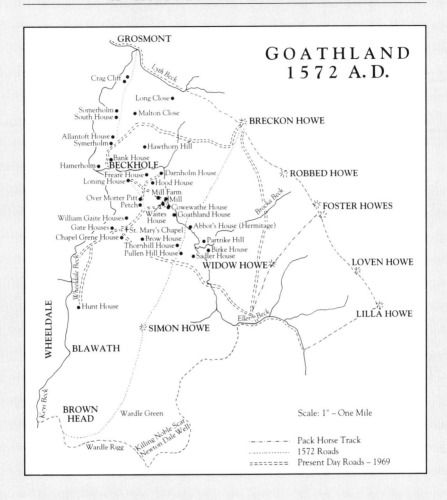

GOATHLAND
1572 A.D.

GROSMONT

Lyth Beck

Crag Cliff ●

Long Close ●

Somerholm ●
South House ●   ● Malton Close

BRECKON HOWE

Allantoft House ●
Symerholm ●   ● Hawthorn Hill

Hamerholm ●   ● Bank House
BECKHOLE
Freare House ●   ● Darnholm House
Loning House ●   ● Hood House

ROBBED HOWE

Over Morter Pitts ●   ● Mill Farm
Petch ●   ● Mill
● Cowewathe House

Brocka Beck

FOSTER HOWES

William Gaite Houses ●   Waites
House   ● Goathland House
Gate Houses ●   ● Abbot's House (Hermitage)
Chapel Grene House ●   † St. Mary's Chapel
● Brow House   ● Partrike Hill
Thornhill House ●   ● Birke Hill
Pullen Hill House ●   ● Sadler House

LOVEN HOWE

WIDOW HOWE

LILLA HOWE

WHEELDALE

Wheeldale Beck

● Hunt House

Eller Beck

SIMON HOWE

BLAWATH

Keys Beck

BROWN
HEAD   Wardle Green

Killing Noble Scar
Newton Dale Well

Wardle Rigg

Scale: 1" – One Mile

— · — · —   Pack Horse Track
· · · · · · · ·   1572 Roads
========   Present Day Roads – 1969

The only thing Goathland lacked for its self-sufficing economy was salt. During good weather a journey had to be made to the Whitby salt pans, for in autumn the salting down of surplus carcases must be done. Only those animals which could be expected to survive on the gathered hay, rough herbage, straw and tree loppings could be kept through the winter.

Although timber on the forest land had diminished with the years, much ground was still covered by woodlands of oak and ash.

The Duchy farms and cottages were 'let at will' and held as hereditary possessions through successive generations. The rents were very small and by Elizabethan standards the management of the land was left to the tenant who ploughed it and cropped it as if it really had been his own.

The first essential for the Tudor farmer was to acquire enough land to grow corn and other things for his family's food and for his cattle, whilst having some to leave fallow for the next season's sowing because it could not bear a crop every year. The best, driest and sunniest places had been taken into cultivation first and other land usually became pasture. It took at least two acres of such land to summer feed one cow. Unploughable slopes and wetter land were used for meadow with the herbage from hedgerows and thickets thrown in. The manure, such as it was, all went to the arable, but it was poor, for meadows mown year after year without remission became unproductive making less winter feed. Pasture grew thinner under the old farming methods; it was a vicious circle, no headway being made.

A mixture of wheat and rye was sown together in autumn, about two or three bushels to the acre scattered broadcast. In a good season a five-fold yield could be expected.

Barley, oats and pulses were sown in the spring. The harvest then as now, depended on the weather, but a bad season or wet harvest weather meant the difference to them between having enough food and being pinched even to starvation. Luckily oats grew well and porridge is filling and nourishing. Rye was also grown and could be mixed with a little wheat or barley. In bad years beans and peas were ground up and mixed in; acorns were used in extreme hardship.

Oxen were used for ploughing for almost two hundred years longer, perhaps because they are easier to feed in winter. An ox can live and work on rough fodder and will eat almost anything, existing where a horse could not.

Tom Keld's Cottage

Over Mortar Pitt House, built around 1520
and last used in the 1920s.

The routine of the land changed little. Daily life continued year after year in much the same way. In Queen Elizabeth's time, hours of work were settled by Statute — 5 a.m. to 7 p.m. in summer during haytime and corn harvest and 7 a.m. until 5.30-6 p.m. in winter, but a farmer scarcely needed reminding to make full use of the daylight. Today, these hours may seem excessive but they were normal on the land in Goathland until the First World War, six days a week.

Henry VII tried to stock Pickering Forest as it had been in earlier times when hunting was the principal use of forest and waste, but in later Tudor times attention was directed to increasing the income of the Duchy. Many acres of land, cultivated and waste, were leased and the lessees had to make what profit they could out of the occupiers.

Sir Richard Cholmley was the first lessee. He ordered all Goathland tenants to enclose pieces of waste. About seventy acres were taken in, much of it of little worth. The average rent was 4d an acre. To the horror of the easy going farmers he altered the whole method of letting the farms and cottages — making each for one life only. Perhaps the dire possibilities with which this order was fraught caused the peasants to exert themselves. To take a long view over the economy of the next century shows that about this time an increase in production beginning in a small almost imperceptible way expanded gradually.

It was fortunate for the community's self-sufficing economy that iron was found both on Allan Tofts and on the moor behind the church. It was a commodity no farming area could manage without. Though tools were of the simplest kind, the dig or iron spade, the gripe or fork, the gaulocke or crowbar, the trimming of the plough, all needed iron. Harrows varied from thorn bush to home-made ash toothed ones, yet before long one man had 'a harrow with Ireon teeth'.

There were fields of two or three acres set aside for the blacksmith and shoemaker, and no doubt they bartered their work for help with the ploughing, the one making tools, the other whittling out clogs from the alder trees which filled the valleys, or using the valuable hides of winter killed beasts for shoes.

Goathland was well-wooded, and Sir Richard Cholmley appropriated one hundred and twenty oaks for building a gallery in his new house at Roxby near Thornton Dale. He plundered the best trees, had them de-barked, the bark being saleable to the tanners, and the branches stripped. The wood and trunks were taken to George Barnard the village carpenter. There they were suitably sawn, adzed, mortised and tenoned, and holes were bored to take the wooden pins which would hold the framing together. The account says 'they were sawn and framed in Goteland by one George Barnard, a wright and those who wrought with him', before being taken to Roxby.

In small places a bit of interesting scandal is always exciting. The villagers discussed the repeated warnings sent to William Harbot about felling trees without permission. Doubtless he needed them to build another house and barns. William had come, probably to Pullen Hill, about 1554, a man of determined and stubborn character, but it was the foresters duty to cut and give timber if wanted by tenants. As they did not do so, William continued to help himself though he had neither any right, nor the authority of Sir Richard.

At last John Bradyll, Surveyor of Her Majesty's woods in the North was so exasperated that he pleaded the Chancellor of the Duchy to intervene. In part, this pleading records that William 'entered into the Quene's Majesties woods and then and there, has cute downe with his awne hands 4 score oaks without any warrent, and converted them to his awne use.' The record is clear enough, and when opportunity came he bought both Pullen Hill and what must have been the new house, Sadler, for £200.

About this time it was Goathland's turn to have its woods reviewed. The inspection was thorough. Trees in the woodlands, depleted today but still known by their Elizabethan names, were seen, counted, described and valued. It had been the policy to plant oak and ash in the quickthorn and crabtree hedges round the fields, whereby the tenant might obtain small wood as handles for implements or for gates. Every tree in the farm hedges was noted and valued. Today where ancient hedges have been removed to accommodate modern machinery, farmers have left oak and ash trees once growing in them, indicating this old custom.

A report of a Commission called to review the intakes and common land in Goathland shows that compassion and humanity existed at a time when poverty was accepted.

Until the Dissolution of the Monasteries the priest had accommodation at Abbot's House, with the field known as Chapel Hill to work. When the house and farm went into private hands after 1539 he would be homeless and landless. Sir Roger Cholmley, with the consent of the Queen, allowed the priest to occupy a 'parcell of grownde in the crowke of the becke... without rent payinge.' The same document tells of another charitable act:

> 'there is also a Lyttel cottage besides the chappell with a Lyttel parcell of grownde for a garthinge which one old ... woman doith dwell in for charytes sake of the sufference of Sir Richard Cholmley without rent payinge.'

In 1572 Goathland was leased to Maurice Barkley. On an enquiry into this lease the names of all the farms, and their occupiers and Crown rents were set out. Since most of the farms retained their Elizabethan names until the 19th century it has been possible to construct a map showing where the occupants lived. There were thirty-three names on the list. One man occupied a cottage for 4d, about six or seven cottagers had small holdings, and the remaining farms were of varying sizes, the largest being on the ancient land of Somerholm at Green End.

Most of the houses were built on a cruck, or fork structure, but details are only available for one such building. Thirty-six oaks were given according to the ancient custom of *housebote*, to construct three pairs of crucks, posts and beams. This made a house of two rooms end to end, each about 14 ft. long. In one of these the family cooked, ate and sat. It was called the forehouse. The other was called the parlour and was invariably used as a bedroom, often containing several beds. It was a storage place too, for butter churns, cheese presses, kimlins, milk bowls and so on. If the house was built on two pairs of crucks it contained only one room.

Glass was rare and expensive, so it is unlikely there was any in Goathland. Light had to be admitted, at least to the forehouse where work was done, so a hole was left in the wall, trellised with wood, and when necessary closed with a shutter.

Families were used to living in a dim hazy atmosphere. The chimney, often a short construction of stone slabs opening on the thatched roof below the ridge pole had at first, an iron rod fixed in it from which a hook hung to carry kettle and pot. Later, an iron arm with several hooks or reckons swung from the side over the hearth which was at floor level.

The floor was earth pounded hard, good, but apt to get muddy in the doorway. In later times floors were paved with flagstones, but earth floors remained in some places until the turn of this century.

On the entrance side of the fireplace was the high-backed wooden or stone seat, called a settle, keeping draughts at bay, enabling three or four people to toast their toes. There were no chairs, only wooden forms and stools. The table was frequently of the tressle type, removable when space was needed. A wooden chest served to keep extra clothing and bedclothes.

In both the one and two roomed houses a ladder led to a floor under the thatch which was used for storage or extra sleeping place. There was no other accommodation in the house. Cold blew through it, but inside as well as out-of-doors the inhabitants were inured to cold, their only cosiness was a short time for fun and laughter as they gathered round the remains of the fire, carding wool, spinning, whittling away at wooden tools or utensils before weariness sent them to rest. Their clothing was of coarse hemp or wool, hand spun and woven, never warm enough to keep out the cold. It soon became dirty too. Nowhere in England was it an era of great cleanliness, but the woman at Goathland had small chance of keeping clean. Water had to be carried, often long distances from stream or spring and heated over the one turf fire. Her scanty supply of soap was concocted from tallow and wood ash.

The baby was washed at birth, the corpse at death. In between, a wash all over was an unusual occurrence. Men and children washed in the cold trough water when mud made ablutions necessary. Clothing was rarely washed. The wood ash soap served to cleanse the coarse hempen fabrics which were a muddy brown colour anyway. Wool would be made clean with urine.

The woman's work like her husband's was long and hard: baking her coarse bread on the hearth, milking the cows, making butter and cheese, spinning the wool and brewing the beer. She would attend the onions, leeks and cabbages growing in her garden, extract verjuice from crabapples, make tonics and salves from herbs and wild plants, bring in wood and turf, and make the best use of everything she could procure. Nothing must be wasted.

Besides all this there was the problem of child bearing. A woman depended on her neighbours to tide her over this period, to take the other children, to feed the husband. If the birth was too difficult or the hygiene too inefficient the woman died, and generally the baby too.

Within a few years of the accession of Queen Elizabeth the new Church of England was firmly established and, by law, services must be attended on Sundays and Holydays or the people who refrained were fined 12d. The money was collected by the Churchwardens for the relief of the poor.

The ancient chapel was small and insignificant in looks, its roof covered with thatch. It stood on the common surrounded by the Chapelgrene. About 1570 churchwardens were ordered to remove their stone altars and replace them with movable Communion tables, so Goathland's was put outside the door on to the Chapelgrene. Grass grew over it and later a grave yard was enclosed. It was found again centuries later when a grave was being dug. It now stands in the north-east corner of the present Church.

THE SEVENTEENTH AND EIGHTEENTH CENTURIES

nly two farms were in private hands at the beginning of the 17th century. Abbot's House, once the Hermitage (and never a possession of the Duchy) was now owned by the Bushell family of Whitby, and Hunt House belonged to Katheryn Ratcliffe.

In 1604 King James granted the lease of *Goteland* to Sir Robert Cary and John Barton for the sum of £944.5s.0d. The fee-farm rent for which they were responsible to the King was £21.8s.4d. After some negotiation Goathland was sold to Sir Robert and his brother George. They then sold eleven or twelve separate farms, principally to the occupying tenants.

Sadler House and Pullen Hill House were sold to William Harbot. Birk House to Lawerence and Matthew Knaggs, Goathland House to the Barnards. Goathland Mill, Cow Wath, Thornhill, Partridge Hill, Allan Tofts Farm and Beckhole were also sold. The remaining farms were let to customary tenants as before.

During the first part of the 17th century there was a tremendous striving for greater prosperity on the land, all profits being put back into the farms, none being spared to improve the comfort or size of the house or the living of the inhabitants. This in many cases could have been a direct consequence of the land sales. Improvements could be made with no fear that the better cultivation and superior crops would be penalised by increased rent. When all round prosperity came human comfort would be improved.

Women as persons were of little account. Their work for the household and on the land continued without ceasing year after year, but apart from being registered at baptism and recorded at death they went through life without status. Sometimes their names are missing from the marriage registers, e.g. 'Phillipe Boyes was married 24th of May, 1661. John Chapman was marryed Furway (probably February) the 29th, 1662.'

When their children were brought to the chapel for baptism, only the father's name was mentioned, e.g. '1600. Geo. s. of Thomas Grayson was Baptised ye XXth Day of Aprill.' This naturally established who was economically responsible for providing for the child.

In 1615 a Record of Ale House Keepers in the North Riding shows three people licensed here. Evidence suggests that George Sleightholme may have been Innkeeper at the *Wayside Inn* near Abbot's House, which had sprung up when the hospitality of the Hermitage vanished. Thomas Monkman may have had the *Chapel Inn* (later *Cross Pipes*) and William Bickers the *Beckhole Inn* (later the *Lord Nelson*). The three new licensees were brought before the Justices of the Peace in 1616 for selling ale above the proper prices.

The village was fortunate to have the spiritual guidance of a young and vigorous pastor called at his Induction in 1626 'a man known for his good life, conversation and behaviour and for winning people to the Zeale of God's Worde.' William Boyes gathered the villagers around him. Before long they had asked and been granted permission by the Dean of York to bury Goathland dead at Goathland instead of Pickering. The roads over the moors were still mere tracks. Strangers wishing to cross in any direction had to engage local guides, and even to natives, passage in winter was difficult, so it is not unreasonable to suppose that burials had already taken place on the Chapelgrene.

As an aged man this minister was a follower of George Fox, introducing him into Goathland Chapel which Fox refers to as 'the old priest's steeple house in the moors.'

The Civil War which ravaged so much of the North Riding seems scarcely to have touched the village, but one of its sons, Christopher Simpson of Hunt House served the King in the Duke of Newcastle's army. His story is told more fully in the Chapter 'Wheeldale and Hunt House'.

Another youth left not for war but to pursue a career of commerce in London, where he became a vintner. He was John, the elder of the two sons of Christopher Barnard of Goathland House. Edmund, the younger, helped his father to farm the land. In 1737, John's youngest son, also called John, became Lord Mayor of London.

Around the middle of the 17th century wool production from the moorland sheep had increased beyond what could be used by the families. Every farm and cottage had its spinning wheel, some had several, but the weavers looms were operated mostly in the cottages, so this industry grew up alongside agriculture. There was a felt maker at Beckhole using up small locks of wool by beating them with glue, and also a skinner. Since a number of glovers worked on Egton Side it may be that this skinner, Paul Snawdon, prepared the leather for them.

Before shearing, the sheep were washed in the beck. One of these washbecks with its bields still remains on the Eller Beck above Gate Houses. While a man held the sheep in the running water, another rubbed the wool. Shearing was a skilled job; neighbours joined each other, and then as now it was a jolly occasion. The fleeces were removed whole and tied up with their own wool.

Two fulling mills were built, one on the Eller Beck at Darnholm, the other on the Murk Esk at Beckhole to deal with the woven cloth. Both at Darnholm and at Green End above Beckhole were fields which still bear the name Tenter, where cloth from the fulling mills was stretched over frames to dry.

At the time of the Commonwealth, a Survey of Goathland Intakes was made with the object of increasing the income. The investigation was concerned with 157 acres of what had once been common land which lay intermingled with the farm lands. The holders had previously paid very small annual sums as rent but on what the Surveyors called 'Improvements' the land was said to be worth twenty or thirty times as much. Names of the occupiers, acreages and the old rents are set out alongside the newly recommended rents. Despite the fact that Goathland farming was gradually improving in every way, that is in numbers of cattle, sheep, amount of available manure, and seeding, the new rent must have been truly discouraging, although the comment in the North Riding Parliamentary Surveys was that the price of 4s.3d. per acre at which it worked out, was only slightly above the average.

Some of the Goathland farmers objected, saying they had these intakes as part of the land they held in *fee-farm*, but the Surveyors would have none of it since they found the intake rent was paid as distinct from the *fee-farm* rent.

The population between 1520 and 1620 increased only by eight households to thirty-seven, dropping again to thirty-three by 1664 when the first Hearth Tax was collected in the village by John Cockerill, Constable for that year. He wrote the names on a scrap of paper which can still be seen at the Public Record Office. Only one house had two hearths, this belonged to 'Mr' Peirson, the title showing he was greatly respected. It also means that up to this time the expected prosperity on the land had not yet reached the point where homes could be rebuilt on a larger and more comfortable scale. During the next ten years the number of houses reached forty-one, but afterwards there were bad harvests and many barren years when poverty increased on the smaller farms, and the number of poor and destitute grew, causing more affluent men to think gravely of some way to overcome it.

In 1685 there were forty-three households but two were excused payment of Hearth Tax on grounds of poverty. Forty-one paid, but even then there were still thirty-four of the old one-storey two-roomed dwellings with one fire for all purposes.

In 1743 in Archbishop Herring's Report, the priest here gave the number of households as 'forty-four of whom one is Popish.'

There was no road over the moor via Eller Beck from Pickering — there were too many difficulties to cope with, though undoubtedly there had been a track for centuries.

The main road between Whitby and Pickering lay via Abbot's House and Simon Howe. It was very poor, over rutted tracks among the heather, in summer baked hard and bumpy, in wet weather slippery in a slough of mud. It was easy to lose the way. People unfamiliar with it had to be guided for there were no signposts and few way markers. Probably the causeways still to be seen were built through the village about the middle of the 17th century.

Parish officers got no pay. They were elected for one year, dutifully performing the requirements of their office knowing someone else would take up the burden when the year was finished. The oldest and principal officials were the churchwardens with civil as well as ecclesiastical duties. The overseers of the poor relieved the aged, dealt with illegitimacy, built a house — or houses — on the common land for the homeless, and when money for the poor was left in wills, as was by no means uncommon here, used it for charitable purposes. They were authorised by the Justices of the Peace to levy a poor rate, submitting their accounts to them yearly.

There was a growing number of poor whose lives were at bare subsistence level, mostly still living in old one roomed dwellings. Responsible people in the village were troubled, and times were unlikely to get better quickly. In

1739 and 1740 very poor harvests resulted in a rapid rise in the price of corn. There was scarcity, almost famine, everywhere. The Justices took the unusual step of ordering the Custom House officers at Whitby to open their port for the importation of foreign rye because 'rye has been above 5 shillings per bushel for three weeks past.'

In 1739 Goathland levied a poor rate of 6d. in the pound which brought in £10. It appears from the Poor Rate Assessment Book which continues until 1803 that a very varied character of relief was available, but for several years help seems to have been chiefly provision of fuel, rent and clothing.

A house was built upon the common near the Chapel for a homeless woman and is recorded as follows: 'Be it remembered that the tenement now in the possession of Isabella Prust and situated near the Chappell in Goathland doth belong unto the poor of the same Township.'

As the century drew towards its end more people asked for relief, the Assessment becoming 2s.6d.

A maimed Militia man, his wife and two children were a continual expense over many years. Another family living in Yedingham whose place of birth seems to have really been Goathland was moved here in a completely destitute condition. A house with furniture and bedding was supplied, and over a long period food, clothing, fuel and all the family needs were provided.

Medical attention could be obtained. It may be that the air of Goathland is a tonic in itself that there is only one such entry, i.e. 'Paid Geo. Wrightson for curing Dunn's two children £1.11s.6d.' The sum received for this was substantial and it would have been interesting to know what the illness was.

A small holder of six acres died leaving his wife with two little children. The overseers paid her rates, rent and land tax, repaired the house, ploughed the land, mowed the grass and dug fuel for her for eight years. Even so, this family lived in poverty unimaginable today.

Because of its nature most of the stories in the Poor Rate Book are sad, but twice happy events were recorded. On each occasion a couple in poor circumstances wished to marry for which a journey to the church in Pickering was necessary. The overseers provided the necessary conveyance and catered for the old village custom 'running for the bride's garter' not at that time a real garter but a ribbon, the possession of which was much coveted by the young men. Several of these ribbons have been passed down in families and are carefully kept today.

The village poorhouse was rebuilt in 1799, the old one being first taken down for 15 shillings by Jonathon Robinson, stone mason. He gives its dimensions in his accounts, 30 ft. long by 15 ft. wide, one storey high and with a partition wall making it into two rooms. The roof was thatched with a mixture of straw and ling.

The thatcher's wage was 2s.6d. per day and his boy 2 shillings. The entire building, stone and work cost £5.19s.3d. Eighteen bushels of lime were obtained from Pickering, travelling on the new turnpike for which a toll had to be paid at Saltergate (6s.4½d.).

In 1763 an Act of Parliament was passed for a new turnpike road via Eller Beck. The preamble to this gives some idea of what a moor road was like.

> *'The High Road from Whitby through Ruswarp and Sleights and over the moors... 16 miles long had been for many years very ruinous, deep and narrow except upon the wide moors which had always been so soft, deep and boggy that in rainy weather and winter seasons, vehicles and even travellers on horseback could not pass without great danger.'*

The Surveyor of the roads, another official appointed for the village, still had to see that the people of Goathland came each year to perform their 'Statute Labour' on the stretch between Sill Howe and Eller Beck. If the work was not carried out properly, the Constabulary of Goathland could be ordered to make an Assessment for the repair. This had frequently happened when they failed to repair the Abbot's House to Simon Howe road.

Farmers were growing more crops of potatoes, rye, clover and turnips towards the end of the century and were acquiring types of manure other than dung. Turf was burnt and the ashes spread, but it is probable that turf ash from household fires had always been used. Marshall writing in his *Rural Economy of Yorkshire* in 1788 says that the Goathland farmers used marl, which they obtained by burning a calcareous stone-like substance from Newton Dale, paying a shilling per waggon load and bringing it three or four miles 'up a winding road over the top of the mountain to Goadland.' This made a valuable manure and brought during slack times of farmwork would be worth the shilling a load. Lime from Pickering kilns would naturally have been much more expensive.

Before the century ended a diligence was running over the moor twice a week between Whitby and York via Pickering. It took a long day to do it leaving about 4 a.m. The cost was 3½d. a mile inside and 2d. outside. In 1795 a coach superseded the diligence, and was possibly more comfortable, but not until 1823 did the Royal Mail run three times a week.

For some time changes in the social character of the village had been taking place imperceptibly. Instead of the old village of one class society, stratified though it was, there now were gentlemen farmers who had bought up farms, yeomen, craftsmen, small holders and, living scarcely above the line of destitution, the poor men who laboured all the hours of daylight on the land.

Thomasson Foss, c.1910

The destination of many visitors to
Beckhole and Goathland.

Darnholm

The cottage of Tommy Leng, the cobbler.

THE NINETEENTH CENTURY

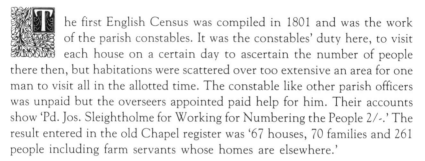

he first English Census was compiled in 1801 and was the work of the parish constables. It was the constables' duty here, to visit each house on a certain day to ascertain the number of people there then, but habitations were scattered over too extensive an area for one man to visit all in the allotted time. The constable like other parish officers was unpaid but the overseers appointed paid help for him. Their accounts show 'Pd. Jos. Sleightholme for Working for Numbering the People 2/-.' The result entered in the old Chapel register was '67 houses, 70 families and 261 people including farm servants whose homes are elsewhere.'

A census recording the number of people here was taken every ten years until 1841 when a different procedure was adopted. The numbers are

1811 — 270
1821 — 335
1831 — 326
1841 — 381

A number of the village tradesmen's accounts are available. Tradesmen, or perhaps better called craftsmen, were respected by the land owning farmers and having had a superior education to the labourers, were looked up to by them. The best start in life offered to a village lad was apprenticeship to one of these, and lucky were the boys whose parents could afford to forego seven years wages of their earnings and let them learn a trade.

All barns, houses, walls and bridges were built of the moor sandstone or freestone, so the stonemasons were important.

About this time the new Eller Beck bridge carrying the Whitby to Pickering turnpike was constructed, the stone being cut by Goathland stonemasons. Jonathon Robinson's account book shows him working for 61 days, cutting stone and 'Wallin by measure, a total charge of £19.12s.6d.'

He worked twelve hours a day, often walking many miles to and from jobs. He charged 3s.6d. per day for his own work with 3 shillings to any assistants.

Several tombstones showing this man's careful and meticulous work can be seen in the churchyard. He gives descriptions of what was required in his account book. A plain roughed out stone which he took from the quarry was valued at 12 shillings. Ornamentation varied, sometimes roses, vases or shields below a shaped top.

Stone troughs placed by the road sides to hold drinking water for horses and cattle were also his work, while others smaller in capacity were used for pigs on farms.

The master joiner shows charges per article when made in his workshop, but if he worked elsewhere it was 3s.6d. per day. A common accident during hay or harvest-time was the breaking of cart or waggon wheels by impact on stone gate posts. He skilfully inserted a new section getting the vehicles into service again quickly, but he made both waggons and wheels when required, and gates, rakes, spade shafts, scythes, plough beams, tubs and tables. The Wardell family were the village joiners for most of a century.

The blacksmith had a forge at each end of the village, i.e. Cross Pipes and Beckhole, and one at Hawthorn Hill, but also did much itinerant work at Peak and the surrounding district. The first of the Swales family, Christopher, came to the district as a blacksmith in the late 1700s, but unfortunately he was lost and died in a snowstorm on the moor at an early age. Others carried on in the direct line until the beginning of the 20th century.

The stone rimmers, one at Beckhole and one at Cross Pipes, used for tiring wheels still lie on the common though there is no blacksmith in Goathland today. He was a versatile man, nothing was too large for him to tackle, nothing too small.

Horses came most days for shoeing. Possibly the boys and men who brought them to Cross Pipes and Beckhole played quoits on the pitches there, while they waited.

No cordwainers accounts have been found although Roger Dobson and Richard Harrison, both of the *Lord Nelson Inn* took apprentices whose names are known and at that time they must have made boots for all in the village.

Ann Swales (1792-1876)

Wife of William Swales, blacksmith

Young farm servants of both sexes lived in where they were employed. Women's wages were £5 or £6 per annum, men had £8 or £10. Labourers received 1s.8d. to 2s.0d. per 12 hour day according to season. Mowing grass, ditching and potato digging brought 1s.8d. Heavy work of sheep washing, shearing or harvesting made 2s.0d. Threshing was paid by the piece: 3d. a stook or 2s.6d. a quarter, beaten on the barn floor with a flail. These wages were poor compensation for hard work yet men dare not refuse a single day, for they had no savings, always living at bare subsistence level. They were men of many skills now forgotten, when Dutch barns have replaced thatched ricks, combine harvesters done away with corn stacks, and wire taken the place of laid thorn hedges.

White bread was a luxury eaten only on special occasions. Brown flour mixed with barley meal was normal. Fresh meat was had rarely but bacon more often, with cheese, potatoes and beans making up most of the diet. Oatmeal, the staple dish at breakfast for a working man, was prepared by scalding the coarse meal for five minutes, when surplus water was poured away and salt and butter stirred in. It satisfied hunger for a long time because it swelled in the stomach.

Many people of both sexes could neither read nor write. The school, such as it was, was inaccessible for smaller children in winter. In summer every child of workable age, that is from seven or eight years onward worked on the land, so except for a few of the very young no-one attended school then. At eleven years old a child was considered old enough to earn its own living.

In 1808 a general meeting of the inhabitants was called to discuss the desirability of a new school in the centre of the dale. Landowners were solicited to assist by 'subscribing to a design which will be of ultimate benefit to their tenantry.'

Certain freeholders were delegated to receive subscriptions, act as Treasurers, superintend the erection and control the building. They were also appointed as Trustees to the School house during their lives.

Labouring people could not contribute money, but the entries in the accounts show they gave their work. 'Six days joiner work, four days mason work, three days with a team, three and a half days hand labour.' All this work which involved considerable sacrifice, since it was unpaid, headed by the money contributions, was 'engraven on a handsome stone and affixed to the Wall in the most conspicuous part of the School Room.' It is there today with its very faded lettering restored by the Local History Group.

Goathland's Churches

The present church, built in 1875
and the 1821 Church, c.1896

Family Christening, 1920

Family Occasion

Holidaymakers join the Underwood family
at the christening of Kenneth.

Three acres of common land were enclosed and let, to bring in part of the Master's salary, the remainder being made up by money paid for instruction.

On 6th April, 1811, Mr James Trenholm was admitted as school master. The Trustees chose three bright children, paid their fees, and the Minutes state 'they were selected by us as Charity Scholars, and ordered to school forthwith.' Many were the boys and girls whose school fees were paid by the enclosure of the piece of common land in 1808, whether they were the Charity Scholars of the 19th century or those of the early 20th.

A new School House, still used, was built in 1875, the sun dial from the old one being placed above the front door.

From 1800 onwards it had become obvious that the village must replace the ancient Chapel. It was very dilapidated and unsafe. During the next twenty years a sum of £377 was collected, a slow task in a poor village. The Rev. Benjamin Richardson and the churchwardens were granted permission to rebuild in 1820. The Duchy of Lancaster made a substantial gift, and on 20th May 1821 the stone mason Jonathan Robinson and his son began to demolish the old building.

The furniture was removed, the two hundred year old oak pulpit taken away to be painted drab, the small silver Communion Cup, the pewter flagons and collection plates, the large Bible, Prayer Book and Homily book stored. The Coat of Arms, at that time beautiful with its new bright colour having been given between the years 1801 and 1816, was preserved, but the ancient font at which for six hundred years Goathland villagers had been baptised, was discarded. In 1841 it was salvaged by Mr Henry Belcher, who placed it in the new St. Matthew's Church, Grosmont.

The church was built in village tradition: the mason being responsible for the stonework, the joiner for woodwork, the blacksmith for making the latch and great key, still kept in the village. Farmers lent their teams and labourers their services. The mason dressed all the stone before building began and erected a course of stone all round each day.

It was a very plain edifice with no architectural pretensions. Above the west end was a gallery reached by a few shallow steps. Musicians both string and wind sat there with behind them a 'singing pew' for people with good voices. Under the gallery was a square pew known as the Baptistry because there, a wooden post surmounted by a stone basin, the whole painted to

Opening Meet of Goathland Foxhounds, 1913

represent marble, took the place of the ancient font. There was no vestry.

The newly painted pulpit was returned, the Coat of Arms rehung, the interior fitted with oak box pews with doors, in which a charge was made for private seats, such payers being socially significant. Last of all a large board headed 'The Benefactors and their Benefactions' was hung upon the wall, giving names of all money contributors to the rebuilding fund, with the amounts. It is preserved in the belfry of the present church.

All the usable wood, stone and whatever else could be salvaged from the old chapel was taken over the road to rebuild the Poor House which had been burnt down. The state of poverty was such that John Collinson, the overseer, determined to build three houses, doing so with the salvaged remains of the chapel, a small sum realised by the sale of a pauper's goods, and by borrowing a few pounds from a villager. It proved a very worthwhile work achieved in the most economical way.

The Tithe Award of 1845 shows the village working 450 acres of arable land, with 600 acres of meadow and pasture, providing food for men, animals and poultry. The intakes were not included in this so altogether there were 1273 acres in some sort of cultivation. It was in 1845 too that a steam railway line with connection to York began to bring goods hitherto unavailable to the inhabitants.

No-one made, or even tried to make, a fortune by farming in Goathland. They regarded farming more as an agreeable and pleasant way of living than as a business. Labour was cheap whether living in at the farm or going daily which many smallholders did. After a long day's work they returned to cultivate the few acres of their holding, sturdy and independent characters who placed great value on freedom, even though it lasted but a few hours.

Tenant farmers lived similar lives, not so opulent perhaps and always aware that too much improvement in their crops and land would result in raised rents. There was fishing in season in the prolific trout streams, shooting, and everyone small and great hunted with the famous trencher-fed fox hounds whose Master and Whip had been village men for 100 years. Lack of a mount deterred nobody in this hilly, wooded terrain; many of the keenest followers went on foot.

The Census Records of 1841 and 1851 show an increase of 70 people in that decade. By 1851 there were 91 houses, a population of 451, men numbering 243, women 208. The excess of men was due largely to workers on the railway. Among them was Henry Goulden, the 'standing engine driver', who lived in the Engine House, and managed the mile long rope and winding drum for the Incline.

From the Census Records too, we find the number of workers needed to run various types of farm. On a farm of 131 acres were two sons of the house, two labourers living in, two day labourers, a farm lad, and one aged 16 called an errand boy. There were three women workers indoors. A farm of 34 acres had upon it the farmer himself, his son twenty-five years old, two day-labourers, and one woman servant indoors.

The horse-ploughing, scythe-reaping, flail-threshing, rick and pike thatching, hedge-laying, ditching done with spade and shovel, took time and labour which was scarcely less than the farming two hundred years earlier.

Children attending school are entered on the Census of 1861. They begin at six years old and continue through to eleven in good numbers. There are a few twelves, no thirteens at all, but one, the schoolmaster's son, fourteen. The leaving age appears to be twelve and it is not until 1875 that a certain standard of attainment was fixed as a leaving age. The new School Board passed a resolution 'that children between the ages of ten and thirteen years are to be exempt from attendance at school after passing the sixth standard'.

Places of birth are also given. It is found that farmers in Goathland then were coming from the surrounding dales — Bilsdale, Rosedale, Westerdale — as well as nearby villages. Railway workers, ironstone miners, whinstone quarry men came from as far afield as Bristol, Bradford, Lincoln, Ireland, Gloucester and Whitstable, bringing to the moorland village a wider knowledge of the world, aspects of life, and qualities alien to the simpler natives.

In 1861 the Primitive Methodist Chapel was built. It was attached to the Whitby Circuit which sometimes sent a preacher but mostly the services were conducted by one of the members themselves. These friendly people with their cheerful singing and sincere speaking attracted many during the following years to their congregation.

Whinstone had been taken for roads of a nearby village without payment for years but apparently it was not used on Goathland roads. The Duchy of Lancaster leased the rights of quarrying to a York firm, and from that time cartloads were tipped at the road sides and broken into suitable pieces

The Day Out

Visitors pausing for a picnic on the Moors, c.1906.

for dressing the roads of Goathland. It was a common sight to see the 'flint knappers' kneeling beside the stone heaps using their little hammers with consumate skill, their 'bait' in red spotted handkerchiefs, with bottles of cold tea lying in the shade of the field hedge nearby.

After it was no longer profitable to quarry the stone a drift was driven into the moor and it was mined. Certain non-village men, hoping to earn larger wages than they could get as agricultural labourers, walked from places as far away as Stape each day. The stone was exploited commercially and cut into cubes for road setts, much of which was sent by rail to West Riding towns.

After the advent of the motor car the industry still thrived but the stone was crushed small in a cracker and used for surfacing such roads as the Scarborough to York road. A good deal went for the making of aerodrome runways during the war. This industry was closed down in 1951 as uneconomic but it had provided work for almost a hundred years.

Socially the most congenial places were the inns which acted in the capacity of clubs and community centres, but for men only. At the *Cross Pipes*, more generally known as the *Chapel Inn*, the churchwardens met to audit their accounts, putting their horses into the parish stable, they ate and drank very abstemiously and charged their supper and 'hoss hay' to the church. At Easter time plays, the old Goathland play especially, were performed by village men both at the *Chapel Inn* and the *Lord Nelson*, Beckhole. These entertainments — joy made for themselves, by themselves — were all they had.

In cottage and farm, life was mostly lived in the kitchen. The flagged floor was ornamented with chalk patterns and a gay hearth rug made from rags lay before the fire. The chairs had patchwork cushions, a settle stood in the chimney corner and almost invariably a grandfather clock solemnly ticked away the hours. There was no water in the house, this usually being supplied from spring or pump, but after 1884 a water pipe was laid down the village from a reservoir supplied from three springs above Moss Slack. In 1893 the Ordnance Map showed six stand pipes by the road side where anyone could fill buckets. These were provided due to the demand of the first few retired or leisured people who had come to live here. The houses had no sanitation indoors. Privies were usually 'down the garden'. Although soon after 1900 a water supply was piped into village houses and into the school yard, sanitation indoors and bathrooms are more recent acquirements.

There was little moving about after dark. Any social occasion arranged in the evening was carefully timed to coincide with moonlight, though a lantern with a piece of candle in it would help in emergency. A great treat was a 'penny reading' or a magic lantern show in the school or Reading Room which was opened in 1894.

Few people took a daily newspaper, but in most homes 't'paper', as the weekly issue of the *Whitby Gazette* was called, could be found. That and the Church magazine were the only reading matter in many homes.

Both postal services and train services were exceptionally good, and the provision of a Reading Room was a great step forward, if only for men.

Probably it is equally as difficult for people today to appreciate the sort of life lived here towards the end of the 19th century, as it is to understand that of Tudor times. Wages were so low it was impossible to save; to keep out of debt and pay for what one could procure was the aim of the labourer and his wife. Today, supplied with an excellent pension it is impossible to conceive the terrible fear labouring people had of ending their lives in the workhouse, or being buried by the parish, hardly a just reward for their lifetime of hard work and frugality.

Popular Rendevous

Beckhole Tea Garden in 1912
when many visitors would arrive by train,
walk to Thomasson Foss and then take tea.

HISTORY OF BECKHOLE

THE FARM

eckhole in the Vale of Goathland has often been called the most beautiful hamlet in the valley of the Esk. It is a small place. Today there are nine houses with a population of around twenty, whereas between 1650 and 1930 when the houses were mostly occupied by families, the children and adults numbered forty or more.

Beckhole! The name is apt. It is indeed a deep hole surrounded on all sides by banks of boulder clay, the bottom once scoured by turbulent rivers. Today, the Eller Beck and West Beck join on its floor, forming the Murk Esk which purls along for the most part. Only at times do flood waters wash over the holmes to the base of that rocky promontory which possibly gave the name to the earliest farm, Amerholm.

But who was the first farmer here? Where did he come from? The answer can only be an informed guess.

On the west side of the valley are little farming settlements with Norse or Danish names — Murkaside, Struntry Carr, Thaksyke (now Thackside). On the east side are the flat lands at the bottom of the steep banks — Somerholm, Amerholm, Darnholm.

About twenty-six acres of land lie in the curve of the beck, some of which must have been cultivated from early times.

The earliest mention of a tenant on the Beckhole farm is in 1572, when William, John and Marryan Ducke lived there. The name of a John Duk comes on a list of jurors fifty years earlier and the family were still in Beckhole in 1621.

Haymaking at Beckhole, c.1905...

...Little has changed by 1932.

A field on the rocky promontory above the low-lying holmes is known asLightening Field or, as the 1845 tithe map calls it, Leighton field. Legend has it that a family named Leighton was given this land and house in Beckhole by Charles I for services rendered during the Civil War. Some say the family came from Fylingdales and it may be true, but there was a family of this name occupying a Duchy of Lancaster farm in Goathland village a hundred years earlier, situated somewhere in the vicinity of the ancient chapel.

When the earliest known sale of a piece of the Beckhole land was made in 1650, the Indenture says it was no longer a Duchy of Lancaster farm but belonged to John and Sara Leighton. How much of Beckhole belonged to this family is unknown today, but it is clear that most of the best farming land was in the hands of a family called Snawdon. The Snawdon farm house was a very short distance from Amerholm, the land reaching over most of the low-lying holmes to a fulling mill on the Murk Esk. Today, on the site is a small house known as 'The Cottage'. John Snawdon with his son, William, worked the land; another son, Paul, dealt with the sheep and is described as a skinner. Attached to the farm and mill were two important moorland sheep strays, one at Langwathside, now New Wath, and one on Allan Tofts at Horsegate Syke, now Hoskin Sike, near Darnholm. The old sheep houses are in ruins though the one at New Wath has been repaired. The fulling mill was leased for three days a week each to separate fullers, the names of at least four being known.

During the 1600s and 1700s the woollen industry was mostly of a domestic nature, carried on in the homes of the workers. Several cottages were built at this time, the women folk earning a small part of the family income by spinning.

William Wilson gathered up the stray locks and coarse bits of wool of no use for spinning. He followed the unpleasant occupation of feltmaker, beating these up with glue in his little cottage.

Weavers of the cloth lived in various places in Goathland village and nearby. The home of one of them is given in St. Mary's Chapel Register as 'Julius Caesar's Park'. It is Julian Park today and is really in Egton parish.

It is not known how long the fulling mill had been working before the first record of it, but its situation is well known. The part of the field in which it stood is still referred to as the 'Mill Steps', though no stone stands on another there today. It was a crossing place with stepping stones over the beck in the early 1700s, for Adam Calvert, the fuller, lived at Murkaside farm and used this short cut to the mill.

Without any documentary evidence it cannot be proved that all the Snawdon land once belonged to the Leightons, but it can be deduced from the *fee-farm* rent paid by the Duck family in 1572 that they worked it all, there being no other farm there at the time.

These first known Indentures bring another of the old Goathland families, the Cockerills, into the Beckhole picture. They had long been influential in the village. Their home at this time was the farm called Twate (Waits House today), originally the Dom le Weyte of 1296, but the first mention of their name is in 1517. Later, just before the Dissolution of Whitby Abbey, one of these Cockerills, Robert, took a lease of Abbot's House (the ancient Hermitage), but such leases were soon declared null and void. Possibly it was this same Robert who was appointed Deputy Receiver of rents in Goathland by Sir Richard Cholmley in 1568, and in 1572 George Cockerill, obviously a prosperous sheep farmer, acquired two farms, Thornhill and Patrike Hill, in order to get the large adjoining moorland strays which went with them. By 1619 the family had purchased considerable land both in Goathland and elsewhere.

In 1650, John Leighton of Amerholm was approached by John Cockerill to sell a piece of Beckhole land of which John's brother Edmund was tenant. They came to an agreement and Cockerill bought Hole Ing and Hole Ing Leases, two fields belonging to the Leightons, with the exclusive fishing rights on this part of the beck.

John and Sarah Leighton were growing old. In 1688 they turned over the remaining land, the oak wood in High Buber and the farm house to their unmarried son, William and daughter, Jane, who were living with them. A year or two later the girl married Thomas Trowlesdale and left the district, but first she sold her share of the house, land and wood to John Cockerill. This left William, her brother, in somewhat of a predicament with both parents on his hands and no wife. During the next year he made a bargain with John Cockerill to sell him his half share of the property also, with the proviso that he should work the land and the old people should have the house as long as either of them lived. Then he married the Snawdon girl next door, finding a pleasant way out of his difficulties.

By 1715, John Cockerill had reached an advanced age and died. He left his Goathland property, including the farm Twate, and all his land and

The Delivery

The Harrisons at Birch Hall Inn, Beckhole.

housing at Beckhole to his eldest son, John, together with an instruction that he must give 10 shillings worth of bread (120 penny loaves) to the poor of Goathland every Christmas. This bequest was a great help to the old and poor for whom there was then no parish relief. A table tombstone to his memory with the bequest upon it stands in a corner of Goathland churchyard. When he died he had acquired all houses and land that belonged to the Leightons in 1650.

During his lifetime he had taken his place in the management of the village, acting as Chapelwarden and Constable in his turn, with, in the year 1664, the responsibility of gathering the Hearth Tax. He also saw the plan for a flagged causeway between Beckhole and Goathland village, though it was not laid until after his death.

A few years after John Cockerill came into his Beckhole inheritance, he decided to rebuild the old house in which the Ducks and Leightons had lived, and live there. The date stone of 1728 is over the door. There is a picture of this house as it was in 1821 on a lithograph of Beckhole made by George Nicholson. With its upper storey and its mullioned windows, it looks a good and spacious house compared with the low thatched cottage which may be part of the old buildings alongside it.

Every house or cottage which now became vacant in Beckhole was bought to add to the Cockerill property. Presently William Snawdon died, leaving farm and fulling mill to John Snawdon his eldest son, a mariner of Whitby. This man sold farm, house and fulling mill to Cockerill.

William Graham, a fuller, was working the mill at this time. Either he retired, and took the licence of the brew house next door to Amerholm, or ran the two together, but it appears that the mill needed repairs, as John Cockerill repaired it and put in new timbers. He then leased the farm for twelve years to John Frank for £12 per annum, with £1.10s.0d. per annum for three days a week at the fulling mill. An interesting part of this lease reveals that the two sheep strays mentioned before apparently at that time always went with this farm and the fulling mill.

Country people in those days had no fruit except what they grew. It was usual for each house to have an orchard of apples, plums, sometimes a pear or cherry tree. If land was scarce, room for apples and plums was made in the hedges. Cockerill planted one large orchard and a number of smaller patches, one of which, under the oak wood at Buber and still recognisable, has always been known as 'Cockerill's folly'. It was truly in an inauspicious position.

Up to fifty years ago, the spring blossom in Beckhole was a glorious and unforgettable sight. Today, most of the trees have gone and few are being planted because imported fruit is so easily obtained.

On John Cockerill's death in 1769, Amerholm was left to his granddaughter, Mary Boyes. The property remained in the family until about 1815, but had been let to a tenant. It was then sold. At the sale, the fulling mill was declared as a ruin and was never afterwards rebuilt.

The respect and esteem in which John Cockerill II was held in the village is shown by the entry of his death in the old Chapel Register as ' Mr John Cockerill'.

The old name of Amerholm has gone, for at some period after his death people began calling it 'Cockerill house'. This is last recorded in the 1851 Census. Later on, the Scots Pine growing near the house gave it the name by which it was known for the next hundred years, 'The Firs'.

The Census of 1861 shows both Cockerill House and Snawdon House empty. The land had been bought by the Whitby Ironstone Company in the hope of establishing a smelting industry in the hamlet. Now the old Amerholm is separated from its land, having been sold as a private house under the name of Brookwood.

RAIL AND ROAD

It was largely owing to the influence of the fulling mill that Beckhole developed into a hamlet with a cottage industry, but by 1793 when William Crossley surveyed the valley with a view to building a canal from Whitby to Pickering, both mill and industry had declined. The plans for the canal were finally abandoned when the difficulty of making the requisite number of locks in the rising ground was faced. Yet help was needed for the port of Whitby, for the once thriving ship-building centre was slowly coming to a standstill. Only an inadequate road service linked the town with its hinterland, and this almost ceased in winter.

In 1831 a plan to build a railway through the valley was put before a meeting of Whitby townsfolk held at the *Angel Hotel*. George Stephenson was asked to report on the financial prospect. From reading his reports it is interesting to find that he saw money coming in from carrying goods of various kinds, but did not visualize any large number of people using the railway.

Beckhole men, chatting in the *Lord Nelson* over their Saturday night pints probably thought of it as another 'wild cat scheme' like the canal. But eventually Beckhole began to buzz with work. The third railway in England was coming through the hamlet. The Whitby Stone Company's quarry on Allan Tofts took on more men, for hundreds of stone sleepers had to be hewn.

Land for the track was principally acquired from John Scarth, owner of the Beckhole land. When the line reached Eller Beck many obstacles had to be overcome, before the work could proceed. A ford and a foot bridge were destroyed to put in foundations for a bridge of Baltic fir wide enough to take the single line. Three hundred yards further along the West, or Wheeldale Beck, the railway planners changed the course of the beck rather than build two more bridges.

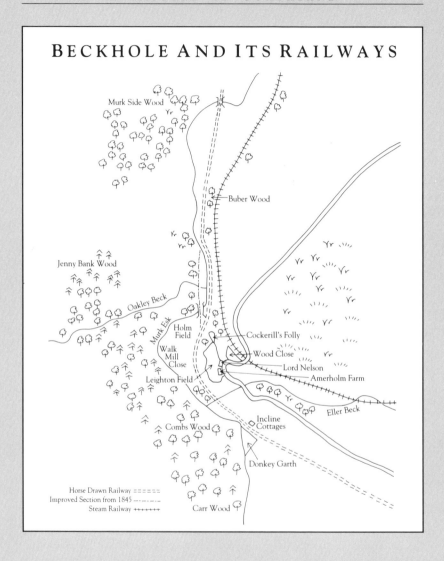

BECKHOLE AND ITS RAILWAYS

Murk Side Wood

Buber Wood

Jenny Bank Wood

Oakley Beck

Murk Esk

Holm Field

Walk Mill Close

Leighton Field

Cockerill's Folly

Wood Close

Lord Nelson

Amerholm Farm

Eller Beck

Combs Wood

Incline Cottages

Donkey Garth

Carr Wood

Horse Drawn Railway =======
Improved Section from 1845 —·—·—·—
Steam Railway +++++++

Nos. 1 and 2 Incline Bottom, c.1910

The railway cottages at the foot
of the half mile long incline.

Next they faced a steep wooded incline. Sufficient trees were felled, the line was laid through a pleasant avenue, but the gradient was too steep for the horses bringing the train from Whitby.

Difficulties were resolved when a large horizontal drum was erected at Bank Top, with a thick hempen rope 1,500 yards long passing round it, and attached to a tank on railway wheels. The other end was attached to the train at Beckhole. Water was pumped into the tank until its weight was greater than the train to be pulled up, and so it descended, with its momentum drawing the train up, the two passing on a piece of double line arranged halfway. At the bottom the water was emptied into the beck.

On Thursday the 26th May 1836 the line opened. Spectators came crowding together to get a good view. The *Lord Nelson* inn keeper set up a refreshment stand and did good business. At last all was ready for what was regarded as a perilous bit of journey. The three coaches, Premier, Lady Hilda and Transit, each with its coachman and guard, were attached to the rope. To everyone's relief they glided easily up the steep ascent. Excitement grew as they disappeared from view in the trees. The downcoming tank was seen and cheered, the entire journey having taken only four and a half minutes.

In 1845 the York and North Midland Railway Company bought the line and changed it to steam. An engine shed and two railway workers cottages were built at Beckhole, with a water pump installed. Alterations were made in the track arrangement and stone bridges took the place of the graceful wooden ones. Now that Beckhole could be reached easily by train, its becks and waterfalls brought visitors to the hamlet.

As the years passed, traffic multiplied and the rope method caused long delays. A permit to make a deviation line granted in 1861 led to difficult work above Beckhole where half a mile of very deep cutting had to be made through a mass of rock and boulder clay. Certain fields belonging to the farm, Bank House, were used, the house itself being re-built higher up the moor. It is now called Hill Farm.

A bridge over the cutting became necessary as the two roads, to Greenend on the left and Hawthorn Hill on the right, were partly destroyed. Roads running parallel with the old courses, which can still be seen, were constructed on the moor side of the new railroad. The bridge is still called the 'Cutting Bridge'.

The rocky sides of this cutting were raw and unstable. Falls of rock and earth upon the line were troublesome and dangerous, so a watchman appointed to patrol the line after the day workers left walked to Esk Valley from Beckhole, then back to Goathland Station to report. If there were excursions or late trains running, a search was made before each one. In the morning another journey was made to ensure the line was safe for the mail train from York at 6 a.m. This patrolling was carried out for around 50 years until scrub and grass stabilised the sides.

Between 1908 and 1915 an autocar ran several times a day from Whitby to Beckhole on Stephenson's original railway line.

The old railway was also used for goods traffic. Engines brought truck loads of goods for the two shops, barrels of beer and cases of aerated waters for the inns, coal for all the houses, and bags of maize, meal and flour for the farms. A gantry was erected to make unloading easier. As there were no means of weighing coal when the truck came for the householders who had to share it, the simple method of taking a cartload each, in turn, until the truck was empty was adopted.

Two severe floods about 1930 destroyed the bridges between Beckhole and Grosmont. They were never rebuilt, and eventually the lines were taken up and sold as scrap metal. Today the original railway line is a much-used public right-of-way which allows walkers, cyclists and horse-riders to explore the route.

The Deviation Line is still in use as part of the line from Grosmont to Pickering operated by the North Yorkshire Moors Railway.

In 1715 an assessment was made for a causeway between Goathland and Beckhole. This still exists.

Parts of the causeway can be seen in several places, though much has been lost by road widening. It reached Beckhole through the snicket on the field side (left) of the present road, progressing down the steepest part of the hill by stone steps.

From early times a wooden footbridge spanned the stream at the bottom of the hill, a ford being used for carts. In 1842 some carpenter's accounts make a reference to 'Beckhole Bridge'.

No attempt appears to have been made to construct a hard road to supplement the causeway until about 1868 when the roadman of that year

All Aboard!

The Whitby-bound train waits at Beckhole Station
which was the terminus for such excursions
between 1908 and 1914.

(according to hearsay, called Morgan) began to cut a way through the boulder clay on Holly Tree bank, and with his shovel and wheelbarrow take the clay to fill in a deep hollow nearer the top of Beckhole Hill, another enormous bank of boulder clay.

Up to 50 years ago the way was known as Beckhole loanin'. (An old house mentioned as Loninge House in 1572 still stood opposite the Water Ark stile, but has now gone). It was only a rough and narrow cart track until after the First World War. Holes were mended with whinstone, heaps of which lay alongside the road, and were broken by 'the knappers' who sat or knelt, their eyes protected by wire goggles, all day long breaking the hard stone with what seemed quite gentle taps.

Today there is a good road to Beckhole, entering by a stone bridge built in 1873. The date of erection is carved on both up and down sides.

The History of Buber
and the
Beckhole Ironworks

uber wood is situated on the north-east side of Beckhole. The name Buber or, as it was first known, Blue Ber, is said to be Danish or Norse in origin, meaning horse or cattle shelter. If this is so, the area would first have been inhabited in about 900 AD.

Buber is first heard of in written history when a Commission of Queen Elizabeth in 1587 came to Goathland to value the trees in that part of the Duchy of Lancaster. At that time it contained 500 mature trees and 300 oak scrubs, and was rented by the tenant George Graison who lived at Symerholm Farm. The house stood on the site of the present two cottages at the beginning of Green End. It is an interesting point to note in passing that, as there was only one farm, only one of the cottages has a commonright. Through this the householder was able to obtain free turf and peat for fuel, heather and reeds for repairing the thatch of his house roof or for his hayricks, and bracken for bedding his animals, as well as the right of pasture on the common land.

The old wood is entered from Beckhole by the gate near what was once the *Lord Nelson Inn* where the signpost says 'bridle road to Egton'. It is said that there was once a flagged causeway down this road and all the way to Egton Bridge. It can still be seen at the gate entrance and in other places for some distance. It appears again on the way to Murkaside where there were once three farms, but year by year it gets more overgrown with grass, as nowadays there is no traffic over it. It has disappeared through road widening on the Egton road except for one or two places where it can be discerned on the hill leading into Egton Bridge. At the turn of the century it was a well-used road to Egton and the farms lying on its route. Every evening except Sunday, groups of men from Esk Valley and Grosmont tramped along it bound for the quoit ground outside the old inn.

Today Buber wood is composed of old and young trees over-run and entangled with briars, brambles, and other undergrowth, but it was not so until the railway divided the Beckhole farmhouse from its land. Until then it was grazed by cows and was a popular and beautiful walk.

Today, as one walks along the Buber road past the bottom of Leighton field with its steep craggy drop into the Hole ing, the banks built to carry the horse-drawn railway of 1836 come into view. The railway had been built down the valley from Goathland to Beckhole and parts of fields belonging to Amerholm farm had been acquired. This divided the farm lands into two parts.

Previously the land from the bottom of the wood to the river was one long stretch, its drainage running into the beck. About seventy yards beyond the cattle arch the embankment made for the horse-drawn railway turns from its straight line, swinging towards Buber wood. Here it is ten to twelve feet high and it seems obvious that much of the stone and earth used in construction was taken from this Hole ing. It appears that the embankment in Buber seems to have been much further from the beck edge than it now is. Perhaps the river during many floods has taken toll of the right bank, or may be the construction and use of the steam railway along the top of Buber wood forced the boulder clay to move down. Whatever the cause, it is apparent that the width of ground now left could scarcely have held the row of thirty-three cottages built for the Beckhole Ironworks and a well-made road in front such as the old horse line was.

———

From 1830, the working of iron in the Cleveland district had increased. Works were built in many places along the coast between Skinningrove and Ravenscar as well as inland. Work began in Beckhole in 1857 when the Whitby Ironstone Company was formed. The following year, the company built houses for workmen and their families, alongside part of the 1836 railway. The firm ground gave them an excellent cart road for the necessary traffic. The part of Buber in which these houses were built took on, and still retains, the name of New Row Wood.

Another house built at this time was known as the Paddin Ken and was built to accommodate the waggoners and their horses. It had a living-room and behind this the stable. A stepladder led out of the living-room to a sleeping loft. Later this was divided into two bedrooms, the stable being made into a back kitchen. It was occupied until 1940, but the back kitchen always retained the name 'stable' and the earth floor. Nothing but the site now remains.

After many initial setbacks, a blast furnace was put in at the Beckhole Ironworks on 8th June, 1860. In Whitby Museum is a tablet especially cast for the opening ceremony with the following inscription:

THE WHITBY IRON COMPANY LIMITED
INCORPORATED
——— APRIL 1857 ———

made the first iron in the valley of the Esk on the 8th day of
June 1860, from which this tablet was cast.
.W.J. Armitage, Esq. Chairman
J. Gill, Esq.   T. Craven, Esq.
J. Cooper, Esq.   W.H. Wilkes, Esq.
J. Whitley, Manager

*Tis the prerogative of man to command, develope and
appropriate to his service the elements with which God has
surrounded him.*

The field in which the furnace was constructed was formerly Walkmill Close, part of the old fulling mill land, but was changed to Furnace Yard at this time. Offices, storerooms and other necessary buildings were put up there.

The boundary of the Ironworks was the Pickering and Egton High Road on the west, extending to the Whitby and Pickering railway and the Goathland beck on the east. Some of the land between these boundaries was farmland and some sloping woodland.

The plan of the iron working was as follows: drifts were driven into the hillsides of Scar Wood, at the foot of which, near the beck, two houses were built. A bridge constructed over the beck took the raw ore to a field known as the Donkey Garth, where it was calcined. Other drifts were opened out in Coombs Wood. In the Donkey Garth all the raw ironstone was burnt prior to smelting. The product was then loaded into trucks and taken by railroad through the Donkey Garth and into the Furnace Yard where a weigh house stood.

Beckhole Ironworks

Model constructed by Charlie Harrison
from drawings made by his father.

The ore was mixed with a calculated quantity of coal or coke to displace the iron with a flux, usually limestone, to form a fusible slag with the earthy impurities present. The mixture was hoisted up and fed into the top of the furnace. At the foot were two holes. From the lower hole the molten metal was run off, while from the other hole came the slag. Above these holes were other pipes through which the blast entered the furnace.

Today there is nothing to show where this took place. Even the enormous banks of slag which built up have now been removed for road making.

But all was not well. The work was unprofitable. On 7th September, 1861, only three years after erection, the property was put up for sale but there was no bid. The works continued to struggle on against the most dreadful bad luck.

First one of the blast furnaces was blown out too badly to be restarted again though work continued in the other until, in 1864, a final disaster happened in Scar Wood. One night the miners went home, leaving their tubs, barrows, shovels, picks and other tools ready to start next morning. During the night the whole cliff collapsed, the workings caved in, tons of treachorous boulder clay and earth rolled down, burying everything. Nothing was ever recovered. This is why the hillside was given the name remaining today, The Slip.

A last effort was made in 1867 to reopen the drifts but it was abandoned. What could be sold of the Ironworks plant was disposed of. Four cottages, two in Beckhole, two on the hill top above, were built from the tall chimney and offices. The engine house was dismantled and taken to Grosmont, by Mr James Harrison, for a joiner's shop and premises. The occupants of the houses in New Row got other work, some in Grosmont, some in other places in the Esk Valley where iron mining was more successful. When they all became vacant, the Railway Company bought the stone and removed it to Malton.

Slowly nature began to cover the scars on the hill sides. Brushwood grew up, primroses, forget-me-nots, red campion and grasses of all sorts sprang up in the ruins. Wild strawberry sent its runners over the slag heaps. Beckhole said good-bye to its 'Iron Age' and went to sleep again in the sunlight.

After the plant was dismantled, an ex-employee, Mr Charles Harrison — late of the *Birch Hall Inn*, Beckhole, but brought up at the *Lord Nelson* where his father, 'Black Dick', was host — made drawings to show what the ironworks looked like.

The Industrial Revolution only touched Beckhole for a brief period, but it must have been a bleak time for the workers and their families who came from various places in England — even the extreme south. At first, the women were pleased to see the new little stone-built houses with their neat living-room, scullery and two bedrooms. Then they looked at their surroundings and were appalled.

Those who had previously lived in villages or towns near iron works felt their hearts sink at the barrennness and loneliness of the countryside around. Even the great hills surrounding them seemed to bear down and shut them in. They could just see the blast furnace chimney but apart from that there was not a single building to be seen except one farmhouse peeping over the top of the almost perpendicular hill behind them in a place they were told was Green End.

Frequently there had been a school their children could attend. This kept them out of the way and they were safe and moderately warm inside. Among the mothers were some who hoped the young ones, especially the boys, would learn to read and write and have a better chance in life. As for the girls, they must at least learn the womanly arts — mending, knitting their own stockings, even sewing new clothes if any material was forthcoming. But here in this desolate place was no school, no shop, no place of worship, just nothing! Their only cause for thankfulness was that the family had a roof over its head and their husbands had found work again.

In Beckhole they found a little shop which sold them flour to make bread. They were promised a shop near their houses in Buber, and in due course, a shop was opened by William Underwood, first heard of in the district at the time of the 1851 Census as a young lodger, described as farmer and victualler, at Julian Park.

The Rev. Henry Wilkinson, Vicar of Grosmont was very concerned by the plight of the newcomers. He asked permission from both the Railway Company and the Ironworks that people should be allowed to walk down the side of the railway track to church and shops in Grosmont but met with a vehement no. He pointed out that the district was very hilly, the roads bad and so circuitous that any other way was almost impossible, adding miles to the distance, but it was of no use. However, on hearing this, the men scrambled up the hillside behind the houses, making a trackway through the briars and brambles to the top of the hill at Symerholm farm where they could reach the Green End road. It was so narrow and steep that it was called the 'cat walk' by which name it is known to the older locals today, though there has never been any real cause to use it since the 1864 railway was built and a road and bridge made. A long way round, true, but easy walking.

There was a narrow roadway between the bottom of the hillside and the cottages, with a wide road for carts in front. One can still see the path made by the women to the beck as they went for water. In those days it was clean and fresh, fit to drink. Whether at first they had any other supply than this is uncertain, but some years later a stone trough was placed at the bottom end of the row, filled from a spring on the hillside above. Its overflow formed a narrow, stony gutter which has to be crossed on the walk down today.

Probably the sanitary arrangements were crude. It was usual to provide two or three earth closets for a row of such buildings. There were no gardens, but at a later date some of the inhabitants received permission to keep a pig in a part of the wood nearer Beckhole. The ruins of these pigsties are still there among the brambles.

Pretty soon, the persistent Vicar of Grosmont was allowed to use one of the empty cottages for a Sunday service arranged for seven o'clock in the evening, so one bit of brightness came into the women's lives. They could take the children, sit in comfort and sing. Presently, with the help of Grosmont school managers, he succeeded in establishing a weekday school for the children in the same cottage, but apparently neither the Iron Company nor the railway authorities took the slightest interest in the welfare of their employees or their families. The Vicar says in a letter to the Ecclesiastical Commissioners that though in 1859 only five cottages are inhabited because the works are not yet opened, he has no doubt that sooner or later an addition of some hundreds will be made to the population, of a class that will add to his labour without providing the corresponding amount of help.

About this time in the north of England some employers, but by no means a majority, began to recognise that their employees were people and tried to help them but evidently this did not apply to Beckhole.

More and more children began to attend the school, including children of Beckhole and from houses in the Green End district. The next Vicar of Grosmont thought a schoolroom should be built onto the cottage. He needed £200 for this but still the works and the railway would give him no help. Although the school was still in use in 1883, it is not known if the schoolroom was ever added. An interesting item is found in the Minutes of a school meeting at Grosmont on 12th April 1870:

> 'It was decided to engage an assistant mistress at a salary of £30 per annum. The fees for infants between three and seven are two pence a week in the lower division. Those in the upper division 2½ pence. Standard one, three pence, standards two and three pay 3½ pence, standards four, five and six pay fourpence.'

A note is added that the present plan is to make the parents find the books, or in default, the committee find a book at ½ penny per week. When there were a number of children from the same family, fees were reduced for the older ones to encourage them to stay at school. This attitude to education was fairly new. Previously children were allowed to leave school when they reached the sixth standard, and as bright children frequently reached it at twelve years it was they who were deprived of further education.

The trains on the railway line just over the beck from their houses were a continual delight to the children. They ran out to watch whenever they heard the long whistle given to warn the smelting works that a train was on its way to pick up the trucks of pig iron. They could see men barrowing the waste slag away to the Great Holme. Years later when thousands of tons of slag had accumulated, it was removed for roadmaking, having served in the earlier years of this century as a grandstand for dog races, horse racing and other amusements and sports.

The people who worked in Beckhole's new industry came from different parts of the country. Mining is work which men usually follow all their lives, or was, until recent years. In the 18th and 19th centuries they moved to wherever they could pursue their particular sort of occupation. The sons of a mining family had no desire, or often no chance except to follow in father's footsteps.

The Census Records of 1861 and 1871 help us to trace the movements of those miners who lived in Buber. They give the names and exact ages, the head of the household, the sex, and relationships of all its members, their means of livelihood and parish or county in which each person was born. The birthplaces of the children show the movements of these families.

At the time of the 1871 Census most of the cottages were filled with families getting their living in some way from the ironworks. There were twenty houses occupied by ironstone miners alone and one by an ironstone miner's widow.

After considering these Census Records, it appears that many workers, especially ironstone miners, had only arrived within the last two or three years. We know that the Scar Wood drifts were never re-opened after the misfortune of 1864, but it could be that this was when the large drift was made in the Coombs with hope of work for many more men. For example, in number twenty-two lived Archibald Murchie aged fifty-two the weighing clerk. The family had only arrived the previous year, from Worcester. His near neighbour, William Blithe had brought his family from Redruth earlier that year.

It is known from a circular which was issued that the Company intended to add two large blast furnaces to the one which remained but there is no evidence that this was ever done. If the one original furnace was still being used it could cope with at least some of the calcined iron but some of it may have been sent to Grosmont or other places for making into pig iron.

There is little left to show the ironworks when one explores the Furnace Yard today, so what became of the fine blocks of hewn stone from which the offices and part of the chimney were built? An interesting little house used for tools or hens in Beckhole shines pink in the sun as it strikes the brickwork which once lined the inside of the furnaces.

Demolition of the thirty-three houses did not begin until sometime in the late 1880s. The only evidence of that time is from Earnest Calvert of Grosmont who died in 1972 aged 83. He said that his family lived in one of the cottages and that they were removed and taken away by the North Eastern Railway Company at the time he was born. He had been told by his mother that the workmen had to wait a fortnight until she was well before they could demolish the cottage. The fact that the North Eastern Railway took the stone away accounts for there being no remains on the site.

One more thing can be recorded and when it was over Beckhole returned to beauty and quietness. In 1890, Mr Wright of Stockton, a scrap-iron merchant bought up all the old iron that remained on the site and had it taken away. He stayed with Mr Underwood at the Firs (the old Amerholm farm) which shows that the land was again agricultural.

The last item to remind the inhabitants of Beckhole that they once had been the centre of an industrial district was a board, its lettering much faded but decipherable, fastened to the wall of the Firs building in the gateway adjoining the *Lord Nelson Inn*. It warned trespassers against entering the premises of the Whitby Iron Company and was there until about the middle of this century.

THE INN

Although there were three licensed inns in Goathland in 1615, their positions are unknown for certain. Beckhole was the last inhabited hamlet on the direct route to Egton, then an important centre for fairs, markets and farming business. It was a convenient and likely place for an inn, but though the names of the licensees of all three inns are known, it has not been possible to find a connection with Beckhole.

The old inn which served the hamlet for over 250 years has been a private house since the beginning of the Second World War. High up on the west front of this house is a date stone:

> 1678
> PB. W.T.
> E ....

The stone was moved to its present position when the old, one-storeyed thatched inn was rebuilt by the Lintons of East Row Brewery, Sandsend, about 1850. The arrangement of the initials on the stone is slightly unusual, but they are thought to be those of Peter Braithwaite. He is known to have held some small bits of land belonging to the Duchy of Lancaster and was also a chapel warden in 1671. Since his name comes in various Hearth Tax records from 1664 next to that of the occupant of the farm, one can assume he lived in Beckhole, for names of householders appear to be arranged in sequence through the village. His name is spelt 'Peter Brahwhat' in the chapel register, the 'E' in the left-hand corner of the stone perhaps being an afterthought of a mason not quite sure of his spelling.

At first, Peter is shown as having only one fireplace but in 1685 he was taxed for two. There is no record of his death so the assumption is that either after an addition, or rebuilding, he sold the inn, for in 1686 the name of Henry Harding, a Pickering man, is associated with it and he certainly kept an inn there. He and his wife, Jane, had three sons and two daughters, but the father died at an early age in 1693, leaving the inn, with its small garth and whatever else he had in Beckhole, to his wife. Though the eldest boy was working, it was a pretty grim outlook for her and it seems fortunate for them all that after two years she married Daniel Faroh of Julian Park (1695) who then became innkeeper. By him she had three more sons.

In their little two-roomed dwelling, with its one chamber under the thatch, there could have been no privacy even if it had not been a public house, but for the next twenty-eight years they appear to have lived happily enough, putting the boys to trades or agricultural labour as they reached working age. Then Daniel died. He left his wife the inn but she was now getting old herself and died two years later.

The son, Philip, who inherited the inn, was by trade a cooper. He employed a William Graham and his wife to manage it. When the wife died some years later the entry in the chapel register is 'wife of William Graham, innkeeper, Beckhole'.

In 1742 Philip Faroh sold the inn complete with a brewing vessel worth £2.10s.6d. to Graham, for £30. Graham, not being very affluent, borrowed the money from William Breckon, a local (Green End) farmer, on mortgage. Trade must have been poor, or Graham was no manager; he never paid any interest and when, in 1763, Breckon wanted his money, both money and interest were still owing. An old friend of Graham's, Matthew Agar, a dyer of cloth from Ruswarp, came to the rescue offering to buy the inn for £40. Matthew himself paid Breckon £35 to cover the mortgage and interest, giving the remaining £5 to the old, and no doubt grateful, William Graham.

Horse riding was the readiest means of travelling on the poor roads of the period, so at this time a stable was added to the inn's amenities. It was built sturdily of stone by the village mason and is still there, used as a garage by the present owner.

In 1781 Matthew Agar sold the inn to Roger Dobson, a cordwainer (shoemaker) and his wife, Margaret. Their daughter, Elizabeth, was Matthew's wife. During the many years of their occupation, the inn was open all night to travellers, food also being provided on demand. In a hut nearby, Roger made or repaired the villagers' boots by day, helping his wife during the evening when trade was brisk. Two later innkeepers, Richard Harrison and William Stanforth, followed the same trade.

Lord Nelson Inn, Beckhole

Despite its apparent anonymity,
this was a popular local hostelry.

The Wayzgoose — the printers' annual outing

Employees of the Whitby Gazette
outside the Lord Nelson Inn, Beckhole, 1904.

It is thought locally that the inn was called the *Bull's Head*, but it is doubtful if any particular name was associated with it then. Roger Dobson's name occurs several times in the Ale House Recognisances, but no name is given to the inn itself until it received a bust of Lord Nelson for a sign. No names for any Goathland inns appear in the Recognisances until about 1800.

Roger's wife, Margaret, or Peggy as everyone in the hamlet called her, was a jolly and friendly soul. She was well-liked by all who called at the inn, whether they were villagers or visitors. These visitors included the Excise Officer who brought with him friends from Whitby and Pickering. Peggy was proud to have the gentry patronising her inn and made them very welcome and comfortable. They on their part obviously liked her and her rather taciturn husband, appreciating her friendliness and good humour.

It was a sad day in Beckhole when it was known that Roger was very ill and on 29th September, 1799, he made his Will, leaving the inn to his wife. He must have died shortly afterwards, because it was proved in the Dean's Court at York on 30th January, 1800.

A paper describes the hamlet in those days as:

> '...... a rural Sequestr'd Valley thro' which winds a clear trout stream over a Rocky Bottom. At the head of the Vale is seen a noble Cascade, and below, a Rustic Bridge. The little Thatched Hamlet surrounded by Orchards is embosom'd deep in Trees. The only Public House in the Village is kept by an aged Widow called Margaret Dobson to whom the Effigy of Lord Nelson was promised as a Sign.'

Any carts passing over the beck used a ford near the rustic bridge. It can be seen, a little damaged by floods, on the upper side of the present stone bridge. The only road from Goathland was the flagged causeway made in 1715 which descended the steep hill by a number of steps to the bridge, continuing through the hamlet past the farm and inn and along Buber on the bridle road to Egton. Such cart road as there was then came over the common and its way to the ford is still well marked.

The occasion of bringing the sign of Lord Nelson to Peggy Dobson's inn towards the end of September, 1801, was well planned. It was to be a splendid meeting of friends from Whitby and Pickering and the people of Beckhole.

A coach ran over the moor from Pickering to Whitby twice a week, but travellers would have been put down at Sill Howe, two miles from Beckhole and ridden the rest of the way.

But alas! When the day came the rain was too bad for the Pickering company to set out. It must have been a bitter disappointment. The Excise Officer and his Whitby party were able to make the journey being only half the distance away. Besides, they had promised to deliver the sign that day and had arranged for dinner to be cooked! Peggy had gone to town on the preparations. Her spotless bar shone, the fire filling it with welcome and warmth. Delectable smells came from the kitchen. Excited women neighbours popped in and out. As for the men, they gathered about the door of the blacksmith's shop opposite — George Fenwick, the fuller, with his partner, Leonard Sleightholme, Matt Ruddock from over the beck, Thomas Linton and William Readman, the stone mason. There was a trickle of others from the village, including Joseph Jackson of the *Chapel Inn* who had always stood surety for the *Beckhole Inn* licence.

When the Whitby party arrived the Excise Officer unwrapped the new sign and showed it to the assembled company. A previously prepared post was brought out and with glasses raised and the King's health drunk, the Officer poured a libation into the earth, depositing a new coin under the post. A crown of laurel was fixed over Nelson's head, then his Effigy was raised and the entire company gathered round singing 'God Save the King' and 'Rule Britannia'. The peaceful little hamlet rang with song.

A poem written for the occasion was recited. It was entitled 'On the Effigy of Lord Nelson being fixed at the door of Mrs Margaret Dobson's of Beckhole being the 22nd September, 1801, the Anniversary of His Majesty's Coronation.' There was considerable play on words as these two verses show:

'No longer so blithe in his workshop he whistles
For Death with rude hand has strok'd down Roger's bristles
For the Soales of the Parish great care he has shown
And we hope he has taken good care of his own.

Life's like an old shoe when all Service is past
Like it we must come to an End at the Last.
For though our old Host was a Comical Codger
We will drink Bon Repos and Adieu to poor Roger.'

Then followed the dinner as good as Peggy and her friends could make

Birch Hall Inn, Beckhole

Martha Harrison poses for the camera in the 1920s.

it, with afterwards, when the rain stopped, a celebration on the Green. The record says, 'Peggy and one of the guests opened the ball and there followed Country Dances, Strathspeyes and Reels.'

After Peggy's death, the inn was kept by her son, John, and his wife, Mary, who brought up a large family there. One by one the children married, except Elizabeth who looked after the parents as they grew older. When John Dobson died in 1877 his possessions were divided amongst his family except that all things belonging to the Beer trade and a certain amount of furniture were left to Elizabeth as if he had intended her to carry on the inn. This was not what Elizabeth wanted. Soon the inn was put up for sale at £100 but there was no bid. A year or two later it was bought by the East Row Brewery, Sandsend, who employed Richard Harrison, a Shoemaker from Egton, and his wife, to manage it.

It is probable that the well-known Beckhole Quoit Club dates from this period, though its most famous victories were achieved around the turn of the century until the First World War.

The inn grew in popularity, trade increased and 'Black Dick Harrison's' pub was a rendezvous for people from far and near. He had a thriving business in the shoe trade too, at a time when country people always had their boots made as well as mended by the cobbler.

Then the Lintons of East Row Brewery rebuilt the inn. They replaced the effigy of Lord Nelson with a painted sign and the whereabouts of the effigy are not now known.

The new inn became a more favourite social centre than ever, especially when the old Goathland Play was performed at Easter. Nobody knows how many times it had been played before 1856, but this was probably the last performance there. It was performed twice a year — on Easter Monday and on Tuesday — but the manuscript of it is unfortunately lost. Undoubtedly, it was of a robust country nature, full of local jokes, with few refinements of speech or action. It took place on the Green in front of the inn where everyone could enjoy it. There was also community singing with well-known dances. The local fiddlers accompanied. Sword dancers, their many-coloured ribbons fluttering, gave dances which included the difficult and spectacular locking and lifting of swords. The entertainment apparently concluded with the 'Cushion Dance' in which everyone took part, the men dancing round the girls, singing:

'We are valiant sailor lads
Who've lately come ashore
And he that delights in a bonny, bonny lass
May kiss her on the floor.'

The boy with the cushion dropped it before the girl of his choice and knelt on it. If the girl approved she knelt also and there they kissed encouraged by the cheering audience, of course.

After the Harrisons left, Mr Thos. Robinson took over; the inn being run by members of his family for almost fifty years. It became more and more popular becoming the recognised centre for Hunt suppers, races, sports and dances.

At the time Randymere Reservoir was constructed and also when the Beckhole ironworks were established, the country farmers and workers found themselves in a less congenial atmosphere. The newcomers were hard-drinking, often quarrelsome, men. It was then that the blacksmith fastened the heavy iron poker to the fireplace to prevent accidents happening when a drunken man tried to pick it up to settle an argument.

During the years when Mr Robinson's daughter and her husband W. Stanforth kept the inn, it was taken over by the Scarborough and Whitby Brewery Company. They presented a very handsome painted sign of Lord Nelson which remained above the door until the licence lapsed.

At this period quoiting was at the height of its popularity. Matches were arranged every weekend and sometimes during the evenings in summer. The watchers who came from far and near stood or sat in silence. The ring of iron on iron was often the only sound on the peaceful hay-scented air.

When the Glaisdale Harriers paid their annual visit to the moors there was a wonderful supper of hare stew for everybody. A local farmer brought down several rabbits to start off the stew along with the first hare that was killed. When the food was cleared and tankards refilled, Mrs Stanforth sat down at the piano. The men sang their own particular songs — it was undoubtedly the men's night!

During the summer, races and sports were arranged. Being a Fox Hunting district, the 'hound trail' was a particular feature. It was laid over the Allan Tofts moor, ending in the Great Holme of the Firs farm.

After the racing the men stabled their horses in the farm stables, the inn stables not having nearly enough accommodation, and the farm horses were turned into the fields.

When the unexpected death of Mr Stanforth took place in 1913, his wife and daughters carried on running the inn for a time, but finally gave it up. Though the inn had one or two more hosts, it declined in popularity and was sold as a private house. The name 'Lord Nelson' is still preserved by the owners.

During the Second World War Algernon Newton R.A. lived in the house which was formerly the Lord Nelson. In order to repay the hospitality he had received from the residents of Beckhole, in February 1944 he presented them with a picture which has adorned the front of the present inn, the *Birch Hall*, ever since. When the owner of the inn sold out to the tenant in 1966, she transferred the picture to Goathland Parish Council in order that it would remain on display outside the inn for both residents and visitors to enjoy.

Padden Ken

Originally the stable for the horse-drawn railway
but later home to the clogger and his family.

A WOODLAND CHILDHOOD

he woodland in the vicinity of Beckhole has been a feature for many centuries. Buber Wood is referred to in a lease of 1572 as a large oak wood.

In 1905 the birch and alder trees of Scar Wood were bought by Mr Emmanuel Moore who owned a clogging business. He brought his family, the three older sons being in the business, to live in the Padden Ken House. Soon the cloggers tents were a feature in the Thackside field now known as Happy Hills. The rough clog soles were dispatched to the West Riding where they were made into footwear for the mill workers. Great heaps of shavings from the shaping machines accumulated and were sold as fire-lighters, at 3d. a sack to whoever would carry them away. The larger ends of wood known as rivings cost 4d. Local lads loaded trucks with the clog soles at 3d. per 1000. ·

The Coombs Wood on the south western hillside is in Egton parish. It was sold and felled. As these trees were large and heavy, being mostly oaks, teams of horses were used for their removal. The trunks were drawn down the steep hillside, and over the Murk Esk into the Furnace Yard. Short ones were loaded onto trucks being sent down the old railway, but for the heavier ones road transport was used, a horse cleverly lifted them by pulley and blocks over tripods onto the lorries.

This wood was not replanted as a whole, but a quantity of quick-growing firs and spruce were put in and felled about 1940, after the outbreak of the Second World War.

Beckhole was a paradise for the children who lived there in the undisturbed years before the First World War. They meandered through fields and woods looking for flowers and ferns, climbed rocks or trees for wild birds' eggs; young ones fished for water newts in moor ponds, older ones for trout and eels in the beck.

Beckhole, c.1920

Plenty of Helpers in the Fields (1930s)

They played games such as Antony, a ball game always played over the roof of the inn stable; Coggs Off, which needs one large stone and several small ones to lead to a deal of fun; Tipcat, played with the stack prods used in thatching the hay ricks, and a tiny piece of wood sharpened at both ends, or using the miniature quoit pitch with real quoits bought and arranged for them by members of the men's Quoit Club.

On autumn afternoons when school was over, gorse bushes which then covered the eastern hillside were cut and dragged to the flat place half-way up the hill from the *Lord Nelson*, where the bonfire had been held time out of mind. Beckhole bonfire was renowned in the district. Naturally very few of the children had fireworks themselves, but bonfire day was also Egton Hirings. Men and maids who had spent the day there came to Beckhole, bringing with them the wonder of Roman Candles, so high and incredibly breathtaking, the fearful joy of Spinning Wheels, Jumping Crackers and Cannons. At dusk the fire was lit, everyone big and little joining hands and dancing round it.

The most memorable of these bonfires took place in a year when one of the cottages re-roofed its cowhouse, giving the old tar felt to the children. The flames grew so high and the sparks flew so far, that the scared adult population had to stand by the various hay, corn and bracken stacks lest they caught fire, but no child present that night could ever forget the awful glory of flames reaching the sky, and bits of the felt, like giant red birds, flying in the wind.

No hay, corn, bracken or turf stacks are seen in Beckhole now. The farmhouse has been sold, the cobbler's shop, the blacksmith's shop, and one inn have gone.

Goathland, 1921

In 70 years little has changed other than the transport.

Photograph by Judges Postcards Ltd. of Hastings.

GOATHLAND IN
THE TWENTIETH CENTURY

As the century entered its last decade the Rev. E.B. Hare a young man of vigorous personality took charge of the church. By his efforts the beautiful and appropriate building now in use was constructed. Pews were free and gradually the social divisions which had become too obvious began to break down. Children were encouraged to borrow books from a small library he arranged in his study at the Vicarage, the very poor were helped, the sick were looked after and no door closed against his friendly visiting.

Quite a number of retired men were building houses. The village became known as a holiday resort too, which helped the cottagers to eke out the still scanty wages by taking in long-stay visitors during the summer months. Each week the *Whitby Gazette* published a list of visitors, where they had come from and where they were staying.

Housework was heavy, all done by hand. On washday water had to be carried and heated in an outside wash-house. Clothes, sheets and tablecloths were poshed in a zinc or wooden tub, boiled in a copper or set-pot, rinsed, blued and starched. Excess water was removed with a heavy wooden mangle. Long lines and props on the common held the clothes to dry. Then sheets were pulled and folded, sometimes put in a heavy press before airing in the kitchen. Other clothes were re-damped and rolled up until the next day; flat irons were heated on the stove or in front of the fire.

Most clothes were of calico, gingham or flannel and women in particular wore many underclothes under long skirts for warmth. It was a common sight to see a woman working with her print skirt kirtled up over a flannel petticoat and a hessian apron to protect the lot. Clogs were worn for work and were hard on hand-knitted socks and stockings, so darning took at least one evening. Knitted garments were made at home but a travelling sewing woman went for days or weeks to make clothes for a family.

Most farms and cottages had a turf fire which was rarely allowed to go out. Each morning it was unsmored (un-smothered). Some dry sticks and a few puffs on the bellows soon produced a new flame. Cutting and drying turf and peat, and gathering and chopping wood were time consuming but economic necessities. Coal was available from the station, but was expensive.

A zinc bath in front of the kitchen fire was filled and refilled from the kettle or side-boiler for the weekly baths. Pans and kettles were still mostly heavy cast iron or brass; a few enamel ones began to appear. The warming pan to air beds was replaced by stone hot-water bottles or a heated brick wrapped in flannel. Children often used ginger beer bottles.

Baking was done at home, quantities of bread, teacakes, scones, pies, cakes and biscuits, but groceries were delivered every other week by the Whitby Co-operative Society in a waggon with six horses yoked two and two together. The butcher came from Sleights with a horse and cart, or on horseback with a basket to outlying farms. Most cottagers kept a pig, which was killed during the winter. The cured hams and sides of bacon hung from the ceiling on great hooks. A branch of holly between them allowed the air to circulate. A few free range hens supplied eggs. When past laying a boiled hen was a treat for a special occasion. Milk was fetched from the nearest farm, and vegetables grown in the garth, or sometimes the farmer allowed a corner of a field for some potatoes.

In the winter evenings, by lamp or candlelight, rag mats were prodded or hooked and patchwork quilts were made from the best bits of old clothes. A Mothers' Union and Girls' Friendly Society were founded at the turn of the century and provided meetings for women. The men had the Reading Room and the Inns. In the winter dialect plays and concerts were highlights for entertainments, and on moonlight nights or carrying a stable lantern, groups of young people walked miles for a dance or a concert. After any seasonal event on the farm: harvest, threshing, sheep shearing or pig killing there would be a 'do'. Life was hard, but rarely dull or boring.

After the Second World War change was more rapid. Mains water and indoor sanitation became the norm. Electricity came in 1948 and to Beckhole by 1952. Most houses soon had a telephone and in 1969 a mobile County Library took books even to outlying places. For a time there was

Looking Forward to the Holiday

Visitors pitch their tents, c.1910.

All Mod Cons!

With a through train from London,
Goathland was a popular holiday destination (c.1910).

a good train service to Whitby and York as well as the buses, but the railway was 'axed' in 1965.

It re-opened 6 years later as the North Yorkshire Historical Railway, bringing hundreds of enthusiasts and tourists to the village. A car park and public conveniences were provided in 1966 and the villagers began to cater for more day visitors and bed and breakfast. The well-marked footpaths, the popular picnic places, the fresh air and amazing scenery draw people from far and wide.

Farms have been integrated, hedgerows have been cleared, machines have replaced horses and fewer people are employed on the land. Housework is immeasurably easier and labour saving. The whole social and economic structure of the village has changed and many retired people have come to live here.

The Plough Stots still dance the ancient long sword dances and bring a model old style plough into the church for a blessing on the Sunday after Old Christmas Day (6th January) but few speak the dialect, and hookey rugs and patchwork quilts are taught as old crafts and hobbies.

One thing remains as it has been through the centuries. At night when the day's work is done the timeless peace of the moors broods over the village like a benediction.

Glossary

agister	a royal forest official who authorised the pasturing of animals on the king's land
assart	land cleared on woods or from waste
bield	stone shelter in the fields
carucate	the amount of land which could be ploughed in one year (80-120 acres)
chase	land reserved for hunting
demesne	land belonging to the manor retained by the lord for his own use. Any tenants were obliged to work on the demesne lands in return for their holdings.
Eyre Court	court held by the king's justices who sat in each shire court once every 7 years
fee-farm	piece of land, or manors held by feudal tenure and services
gaulocke/gavelock	form of crowbar
grange	an outlying monastic farm
gripe	fork
hedge-bote	the right to take wood from common land to make or repair fences
hoton	farm on a hill
housebote	the right to take wood from common land to make or repair buildings
howe	ancient burial mound
intake	piece of enclosed land on the moorland edge

Interludes	drama or mime between the acts of miracle plays or moralities
Lay Subsidy	an occasional tax levied on private property by the Crown usually for military activity
Liberty	area where certain privileges were granted by the Crown to the lord of the manor
loning	lane
messuage	house and outbuildings, and any adjacent land appropriated to its use
Pipe Rolls	account of all Crown revenues, so called because they were rolled around a pipe
Regard	forest court held every 3 years to safeguard the bounds of a forest and the Crown's rights within it
Swainmote Court	manorial court which dealt with petty offences associated with royal forests
tallage	taxation
toft	land where a house stands or has stood
turbary	the right to dig peat or turf for fuel on common land
vert	the right to cut all that bears green leaves in the forest